OneDrive Essentials

Manage Your Files with Ease

Kiet Huynh

Table of Contents

Introduction

1.1 Why Use OneDrive?

In today's digital age, managing files efficiently is more important than ever. With the sheer volume of documents, images, videos, and other digital assets we create and consume, having a reliable system to store, organize, and access these files is critical. OneDrive, Microsoft's cloud storage solution, has emerged as a popular choice for individuals, businesses, and educational institutions alike. But what exactly makes OneDrive such a compelling tool? In this section, we'll explore the reasons why OneDrive stands out as an essential platform for modern file management.

1. Simplified File Access Across Devices

One of the most significant advantages of OneDrive is its ability to seamlessly sync files across multiple devices. Whether you're using a laptop, smartphone, tablet, or desktop, OneDrive ensures that your files are always at your fingertips. This cross-device compatibility means you no longer need to worry about manually transferring files using

USB drives or emailing documents to yourself. Instead, your files are securely stored in the cloud and accessible wherever you are, as long as you have an internet connection.

Additionally, OneDrive's mobile app allows you to view, edit, and share files on the go, making it perfect for professionals who travel frequently or for students who need access to their assignments anytime.

2. Enhanced Collaboration and Sharing

OneDrive transforms the way we collaborate. In the past, teamwork often required endless email threads and multiple file versions, leading to confusion and inefficiency. With OneDrive, those days are over.

You can easily share files and folders with colleagues, friends, or family members by simply sending a link. OneDrive allows you to set specific permissions for each recipient, such as view-only access or editing rights. This level of control ensures that sensitive information remains secure while fostering smooth collaboration.

Moreover, OneDrive integrates seamlessly with Microsoft Office applications like Word, Excel, and PowerPoint, enabling real-time co-authoring. This means multiple people can work on the same document simultaneously, with changes synced automatically. This feature is invaluable for team projects, business reports, or any task requiring input from multiple contributors.

3. Secure and Reliable Storage

In the digital era, data security is a top concern. OneDrive addresses this issue by providing robust security measures to protect your files. With encryption both at rest and in transit, your data remains safe from unauthorized access. Additionally, features like two-factor authentication (2FA) add an extra layer of protection to your account.

For those with sensitive documents, OneDrive's Personal Vault is a standout feature. It provides a secure area within your storage space that requires additional authentication for access. This makes it ideal for storing financial records, identification documents, or any other critical files.

Microsoft's commitment to reliability means that OneDrive is hosted on secure and redundant servers. This ensures that even in the event of hardware failures, your files remain safe and accessible.

4. Cost-Effective Storage Solutions

OneDrive offers flexible storage options to suit a variety of needs. The free tier provides 5GB of storage, which is sufficient for light users looking to store basic documents and photos. For those with larger storage requirements, affordable subscription plans are available, including the OneDrive Standalone Plan and the Microsoft 365 subscription, which bundles OneDrive with Office applications and other perks.

Businesses and enterprises can also benefit from scalable storage solutions, ensuring they only pay for what they need. Compared to traditional external storage devices, OneDrive eliminates the risk of physical damage or loss, providing a more cost-effective and reliable alternative.

5. Backup and Recovery

Accidents happen—devices get lost, files get deleted, and hard drives fail. OneDrive acts as a safety net by providing automatic backup for your files. You can configure OneDrive to automatically sync specific folders, such as your desktop, documents, and pictures, ensuring that your important files are always protected.

In the event of accidental deletion or file corruption, OneDrive's version history feature allows you to restore previous versions of your files with ease. This functionality is especially useful for recovering from mistakes or undoing unwanted changes.

6. Integration with Microsoft Ecosystem

OneDrive isn't just a standalone storage solution; it's deeply integrated into Microsoft's ecosystem, enhancing its functionality and versatility. If you're already using Windows, Office apps, or other Microsoft tools, OneDrive provides a seamless experience.

For example, files saved in Office applications can be stored directly to OneDrive, and Windows users will find OneDrive pre-installed and ready to use. This integration extends to Microsoft Teams, SharePoint, and other collaboration tools, making OneDrive an indispensable part of the modern digital workspace.

7. Environmental Sustainability

Cloud storage solutions like OneDrive contribute to a more sustainable future by reducing the need for physical storage devices, which often end up in landfills. Additionally, Microsoft has committed to operating carbon-neutral data centers, ensuring that your choice to use OneDrive aligns with environmentally friendly practices.

8. Personal and Professional Versatility

OneDrive is designed to cater to both personal and professional needs. For individuals, it's an excellent platform for storing photos, videos, and personal documents. The intuitive interface makes it easy for anyone, regardless of technical expertise, to organize and access their files.

For professionals, OneDrive offers powerful tools to streamline workflows, improve collaboration, and maintain file security. Whether you're a freelancer managing client files or part of a large organization, OneDrive provides the features you need to stay productive.

9. Offline Access and Flexibility

OneDrive's offline access feature ensures that you're not entirely dependent on an internet connection. You can download files to your device and work on them offline, with changes automatically syncing back to the cloud once you're connected again. This flexibility is ideal for those working in areas with limited connectivity or during travel.

10. Regular Updates and Future-Proofing

As part of Microsoft's suite of tools, OneDrive benefits from continuous updates and enhancements. These updates ensure that users always have access to the latest features and improvements, keeping OneDrive at the forefront of cloud storage technology.

By choosing OneDrive, you're investing in a platform that evolves with changing technology, making it a future-proof solution for your file storage and management needs.

In conclusion, OneDrive offers a wealth of benefits that cater to a wide range of users. Whether you're an individual seeking a convenient way to store personal files, a student collaborating on group projects, or a business professional managing sensitive data, OneDrive provides the tools and features needed to succeed. Its combination of accessibility, security, collaboration, and affordability makes it a standout choice in the competitive world of cloud storage.

1.2 Key Features of OneDrive

OneDrive is one of the most versatile and user-friendly cloud storage platforms available today. With its wide range of features, it not only serves as a file storage solution but also as a powerful tool for collaboration, organization, and seamless integration with other Microsoft services. This section will explore the key features of OneDrive in detail to help you understand its potential and how it can simplify your digital life.

1.2.1 Cloud Storage and File Accessibility

At its core, OneDrive is a cloud storage solution. It provides users with the ability to store files online and access them from virtually anywhere. Whether you're working on a desktop computer, using a mobile phone, or logging in from a public computer, OneDrive ensures that your files are always within reach.

- **Cross-Device Accessibility**: OneDrive allows you to access your files on various devices, including Windows PCs, Macs, iPhones, Android devices, and tablets. The OneDrive mobile app is particularly useful for managing files on the go.

- **File Synchronization**: Changes made to a file on one device are automatically synced across all connected devices. This means you can start working on a document at home and pick up right where you left off on a different device.

- **Offline Access**: With OneDrive, you can mark specific files or folders for offline use. This is particularly helpful if you need to access files in areas with no internet connection, such as during travel.

1.2.2 File Sharing and Collaboration

OneDrive makes sharing files and collaborating with others a seamless experience. It offers multiple ways to share files while maintaining control over permissions and access.

- **Customizable Sharing Links**: You can generate links to share files or folders with others. These links can be customized to allow either viewing or editing, depending on your needs.

- **Set Expiration Dates for Links**: For added security, OneDrive allows you to set expiration dates for shared links. This ensures that access is temporary and files are protected over time.

- **Collaborative Editing**: OneDrive integrates with Microsoft Office apps, enabling real-time co-authoring. Multiple users can work on the same document simultaneously, seeing each other's changes as they happen. This feature is particularly useful for team projects or group assignments.

- **Activity Notifications**: You'll receive notifications when someone accesses or edits a file you've shared, keeping you updated on the progress of your collaboration.

1.2.3 Large File Support and Storage Space

OneDrive supports the upload and storage of large files, making it a suitable option for photographers, videographers, and other professionals who work with large data files.

- **Generous Storage Limits**: Free OneDrive accounts offer 5 GB of storage, while paid plans provide significantly more, with options going up to 1 TB or more for individual users and unlimited storage for enterprise plans.

- **Upload Large Files**: OneDrive supports file uploads up to 250 GB, far exceeding the limits of many competing cloud storage platforms.

- **Efficient Compression**: Files are stored efficiently without losing quality, ensuring that your storage space is used optimally.

1.2.4 Integration with Microsoft 365

One of OneDrive's standout features is its seamless integration with Microsoft 365, which includes applications like Word, Excel, PowerPoint, and Outlook.

- **Direct File Saving**: Save your documents directly to OneDrive from any Microsoft Office app. This ensures your files are automatically backed up and accessible from other devices.

- **Version History**: OneDrive keeps a history of changes made to Microsoft Office documents. You can revert to previous versions of a file if needed, making it easy to recover from accidental edits or deletions.

- **Linked Calendars and Emails**: Attach files stored in OneDrive to your Outlook emails or add shared links directly to calendar invites.

1.2.5 Advanced Search and Organization Tools

Keeping track of files can be a challenge, especially if you're managing a large amount of data. OneDrive offers several tools to help you stay organized and find what you need quickly.

- **Powerful Search Functionality**: The search bar in OneDrive lets you find files by name, content, or metadata. You can also search for keywords within documents, making it easier to locate specific information.

- **Tags and Metadata**: Add tags or metadata to files for better organization. This is particularly useful for categorizing photos or business documents.

- **Sorting and Filtering**: Sort files by name, date, size, or other criteria. Filters can help you quickly narrow down your search to specific file types or folders.

1.2.6 File Protection and Security

Security is a top priority for OneDrive, making it a reliable option for both personal and business use. Microsoft has implemented robust measures to ensure your files are safe.

- **Personal Vault**: This is a protected area within OneDrive that provides an extra layer of security for sensitive files. Access to the Personal Vault requires two-factor authentication, such as a fingerprint, face recognition, or a PIN.

- **Ransomware Detection and Recovery**: OneDrive can detect potential ransomware attacks and help you restore affected files to their original state.

- **End-to-End Encryption**: All files stored in OneDrive are encrypted in transit and at rest, safeguarding them from unauthorized access.

- **Customizable Permissions**: Control who can view or edit your files by setting specific permissions.

1.2.7 Backup and Restore Options

OneDrive isn't just for file storage—it also offers robust backup and restore features to protect your data from accidental loss.

- **PC Folder Backup**: You can back up your Desktop, Documents, and Pictures folders directly to OneDrive. This ensures that even if your computer is lost or damaged, your important files are safe.

- **Recycle Bin**: Deleted files are moved to the OneDrive Recycle Bin, where they can be restored within 30 days. This feature acts as a safety net for accidental deletions.

- **Restore Entire OneDrive**: In the event of a major issue, such as a ransomware attack, you can use the "Restore Your OneDrive" feature to roll back to a previous version of your OneDrive account.

1.2.8 Productivity Enhancements

OneDrive includes features that can help you save time and boost productivity.

- **File Previews**: View file previews directly in OneDrive without downloading them. This is particularly helpful for photos, PDFs, and Office documents.

- **Request Files**: OneDrive's "Request Files" feature lets you collect files from others without granting them access to your entire storage. This is great for receiving documents from clients or colleagues.

- **Shortcuts to Shared Libraries**: Easily access shared files from Microsoft Teams or SharePoint libraries directly through OneDrive.

1.2.9 Mobile-Friendly Features

The OneDrive mobile app enhances the platform's accessibility, offering features specifically designed for users on the move.

- **Mobile Scanning**: Use the app to scan documents, receipts, and whiteboards. Scanned files are saved as PDFs and uploaded directly to OneDrive.

- **Photo Backup**: Automatically back up photos and videos from your mobile device to OneDrive.

- **Quick Sharing**: Share files or folders instantly from your phone via email, messaging apps, or shareable links.

By leveraging these features, OneDrive becomes much more than just a cloud storage solution—it transforms into a comprehensive tool for file management, collaboration, and productivity. Whether you're a casual user or a business professional, OneDrive's extensive capabilities make it an invaluable part of your digital toolkit.

1.3 Who This Guide is For

This guide, *OneDrive Essentials: Manage Your Files with Ease*, is crafted to cater to a wide range of audiences who are looking to streamline their file management and enhance their productivity using OneDrive. Whether you're a first-time user exploring cloud storage solutions, a professional aiming to collaborate effectively, or a student juggling multiple projects, this guide has been structured with your needs in mind. Let's dive into who will benefit most from this book and how it can serve as a valuable resource.

First-Time Users

If you've never used OneDrive before or are just starting out with cloud storage, this guide is tailored for you. First-time users often feel overwhelmed when introduced to a new platform, especially one as feature-rich as OneDrive. This guide walks you through every essential feature, from setting up your account to mastering advanced tools.

- **Understanding the Basics**: You'll learn how to create an account, upload files, and organize folders. Each step is explained with simplicity, ensuring that even the most non-technical users can follow along.

- **Building Confidence with Cloud Technology**: We recognize that some people might be hesitant to transition from traditional file storage methods like USB drives or external hard drives. This guide will help you build confidence in using the cloud by explaining its benefits, security features, and reliability.

By the end of this guide, first-time users will feel comfortable navigating OneDrive and will have the tools needed to use it as their primary file storage solution.

Professionals and Office Workers

In today's fast-paced workplace, professionals are often required to handle large volumes of data, collaborate across teams, and meet tight deadlines. OneDrive provides a seamless solution for managing these tasks, and this guide will show you how to maximize its potential in a professional setting.

- **File Sharing and Collaboration**: Office workers who need to share files securely and collaborate in real-time with colleagues will find detailed instructions on how to use OneDrive's sharing options, co-authoring features, and integration with Microsoft Office.

- **Streamlining Workflows**: You'll learn how to automate repetitive tasks, such as setting up workflows for document approvals or scheduling regular file backups.

- **Working Remotely**: With remote work becoming more prevalent, OneDrive's ability to provide access to files from anywhere is invaluable. This guide covers tips for using OneDrive effectively in a remote work environment, including syncing files across devices and managing offline access.

Whether you're an individual contributor or a manager overseeing team projects, the strategies in this guide will help you enhance productivity and stay organized.

Students and Educators

Students and educators alike can benefit immensely from OneDrive. In the education sector, where collaboration, organization, and accessibility are key, OneDrive serves as a versatile tool.

- **For Students**:
    - o **Organizing Study Materials**: Students often deal with a multitude of assignments, lecture notes, and research projects. This guide explains how to use OneDrive to keep files neatly organized in folders, tag them for easy retrieval, and access them on the go.

    - o **Collaborating on Group Projects**: Group assignments can be challenging, but with OneDrive's real-time collaboration features, students can co-author documents, track changes, and ensure everyone stays on the same page.

    - o **Maximizing Limited Resources**: Many students operate on tight budgets. The guide highlights how to make the most of OneDrive's free plan and manage storage space effectively.

- **For Educators**:
    - o **Streamlining Lesson Plans**: Educators can use OneDrive to store and organize lesson plans, presentations, and educational resources, making it easy to access and share them with students.

- o **Fostering Collaboration**: Teachers can collaborate with colleagues on curriculum development or share resources with students via secure links.

- o **Managing Administrative Tasks**: From grading spreadsheets to attendance records, educators can use OneDrive to keep administrative files secure and easily accessible.

Freelancers and Entrepreneurs

For freelancers and entrepreneurs, efficiency and flexibility are essential. OneDrive offers tools that cater to the needs of independent professionals and small business owners.

- **Managing Client Files**: Freelancers can use OneDrive to organize client files, contracts, and invoices in one secure location. This guide provides tips for setting up folder structures that make finding files quick and easy.

- **Enhancing Collaboration**: Entrepreneurs working with remote teams or clients can benefit from OneDrive's sharing and collaborative editing features. The guide explains how to set up permissions to ensure confidentiality while enabling smooth collaboration.

- **Backing Up Critical Data**: Losing important business data can be catastrophic. This guide emphasizes the importance of using OneDrive's automatic backup features to safeguard your work.

Whether you're a graphic designer, consultant, or small business owner, this guide will help you integrate OneDrive into your daily operations for maximum efficiency.

Families and Personal Users

OneDrive isn't just for professionals and students; it's also a fantastic tool for personal use. Families can use it to organize photos, videos, and important documents, ensuring they're always accessible and safely stored.

- **Preserving Memories**: This guide explains how to upload and organize family photos and videos in OneDrive, so they're easy to share with loved ones or revisit on special occasions.

- **Managing Household Documents**: From bills to warranties and medical records, OneDrive provides a centralized location for all your important household files. The guide includes tips for tagging and categorizing files for easy retrieval.

- **Family Sharing Features**: OneDrive's family sharing plans make it easy to provide access to files across multiple family members. The guide outlines how to set up family sharing and manage individual permissions.

Tech-Savvy Users

Even for advanced users who may already be familiar with OneDrive, this guide offers insights and tips to take their usage to the next level.

- **Advanced File Management**: Learn how to use metadata, tags, and advanced search filters to manage large volumes of data more effectively.

- **Integration with Other Tools**: Tech-savvy users will appreciate the chapters dedicated to integrating OneDrive with tools like Microsoft Teams, SharePoint, and third-party applications.

- **Customizing OneDrive Settings**: From optimizing sync settings to using developer tools, this guide explores customization options that allow users to tailor OneDrive to their specific needs.

Small Businesses and Teams

For small businesses and teams, OneDrive can act as the backbone of digital file management and collaboration. This guide covers:

- **Team Collaboration Tools**: Learn how to create shared libraries, manage team folders, and ensure smooth collaboration across departments.

- **Security and Compliance**: The guide delves into OneDrive's security features, including encryption and audit logs, to help small businesses meet regulatory requirements.

- **Scaling for Growth**: As businesses grow, so do their file storage needs. This guide provides tips on upgrading storage plans and integrating OneDrive with other Microsoft 365 tools for scalability.

Closing Thoughts

No matter your background or level of experience, *OneDrive Essentials: Manage Your Files with Ease* is designed to provide clear, actionable guidance that empowers you to harness the full potential of OneDrive. By tailoring the content to various user groups, this guide ensures that everyone—from beginners to advanced users—can find value and transform how they manage their files. As you proceed through the chapters, you'll discover practical tips, real-world examples, and step-by-step instructions to help you achieve your goals with ease.

CHAPTER I
Getting Started with OneDrive

1.1 Setting Up Your Account

1.1.1 Creating a Microsoft Account

Creating a Microsoft Account is the first essential step to getting started with OneDrive. A Microsoft Account provides access to a suite of services, including OneDrive, Outlook, Office Online, and more. This guide will walk you through the process of setting up a Microsoft Account, ensuring you can seamlessly start using OneDrive for your cloud storage and file-sharing needs.

Why Do You Need a Microsoft Account?

A Microsoft Account acts as your key to accessing not only OneDrive but also a broader ecosystem of Microsoft services. Whether you are using Windows, Office 365, or even Xbox, your Microsoft Account ties everything together. For OneDrive, your account is what allows you to upload files, organize folders, share documents, and sync your data across devices.

Key benefits of having a Microsoft Account include:

1. **Cloud storage:** Access your files anytime, anywhere.

2. **Cross-device integration:** Use the same account on your PC, smartphone, and tablet.

3. **Security:** Benefit from advanced encryption and two-factor authentication for account protection.

4. **Collaboration:** Share and edit files with others in real time.

Step-by-Step Guide to Creating a Microsoft Account

Step 1: Visit the Microsoft Sign-Up Page

1. Open your browser and go to Microsoft's sign-up page.

2. You will be presented with two options:

   o **Use an existing email address** (e.g., Gmail, Yahoo).

   o **Create a new Microsoft email address** with the domains @outlook.com or @hotmail.com.

Step 2: Choose Your Sign-Up Method

- **Option A: Using an existing email address**

  If you prefer to use your current email address, select the option **"Use your email address instead."** Enter your email, create a password, and follow the prompts.

- **Option B: Creating a new Microsoft email address**

  To create a new address, select **"Get a new email address."** You can choose either @outlook.com or @hotmail.com for your domain. Enter your preferred username and check its availability.

Step 3: Set a Secure Password

- Create a strong password that combines letters, numbers, and special characters.

- Microsoft may provide tips to improve your password strength, such as avoiding common phrases or using a mix of uppercase and lowercase letters.

- Confirm your password and proceed to the next step.

Pro Tip: Use a password manager to securely store your credentials and ensure your account is protected.

Adding Personal Details

After selecting your email address and password, you will be asked to enter some personal information:

1. **First and Last Name**

   Provide your full name. This name will appear in your account and may be visible to others when you share OneDrive files.

2. **Date of Birth**

   Microsoft uses this information to personalize your account and provide age-appropriate services.

3. **Country/Region**
   Choose your country to ensure access to local services and support.

Verifying Your Identity

To secure your account, Microsoft requires identity verification. This can be done in two ways:

1. **Email Verification:**

   o If you used an existing email address, Microsoft will send a verification code to that email.

   o Check your inbox, copy the code, and paste it into the verification field on the sign-up page.

2. **Phone Number Verification:**

     ○   Enter your phone number and select how you want to receive the code (SMS or voice call).

     ○   Input the code you receive to verify your phone number.

Why is verification important?

- It ensures that only authorized users can access your account.

- It helps with account recovery in case you forget your password.

Customizing Your Account

Once your account is verified, Microsoft will guide you through optional customization steps:

1. **Profile Picture:** Add a photo to personalize your account.

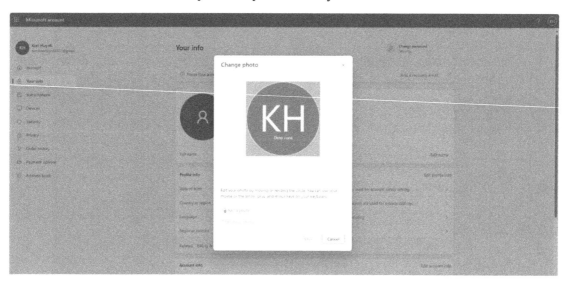

2. **Language and Time Zone:** Set your preferred language and time zone for a localized experience.

Linking Your Microsoft Account to Devices

After creating your account, you can link it to your devices for a seamless experience:

1. **Windows PC:**

   o Open your settings, go to **Accounts**, and sign in with your new Microsoft Account.

   o This links your OneDrive storage to your desktop and file explorer.

2. **Mobile Devices:**

   o Download the Microsoft apps, such as OneDrive and Outlook, from the App Store or Google Play Store.

   o Log in using your account credentials to access your files on the go.

3. **Web Browsers:**

   o Sign in to OneDrive at onedrive.live.com to access your cloud storage from any browser.

Troubleshooting Common Issues During Account Creation

Issue 1: Email Already in Use

- If the email address you entered is already associated with a Microsoft Account, try resetting the password for that account instead of creating a new one.

Issue 2: Verification Code Not Received

- Check your spam or junk folder for the verification email.

- Ensure you entered the correct phone number or email address during registration.

Issue 3: Weak Password Rejection

- Make sure your password meets Microsoft's security requirements.

- Avoid using common words or sequences like "12345" or "password."

Issue 4: Account Creation Blocked

- Some regions may temporarily block sign-ups due to security concerns. Use a VPN or contact Microsoft support for assistance.

Tips for a Smooth Sign-Up Process

1. **Prepare Your Information Ahead of Time:** Have your email address, phone number, and a strong password ready.

2. **Use a Recovery Option:** Add a secondary email or phone number to make account recovery easier.

3. **Secure Your Account:** Enable two-factor authentication after signing up for added protection.

4. **Explore the Microsoft Ecosystem:** Familiarize yourself with other services linked to your Microsoft Account, such as Office Online and Skype.

Conclusion

Creating a Microsoft Account is a simple but crucial step toward accessing the full capabilities of OneDrive. By following this guide, you are now ready to move on to downloading and installing OneDrive, where you'll start uploading and organizing your files in the cloud. A well-prepared and verified account ensures a seamless experience, paving the way for effortless file management.

1.1.2 Downloading and Installing OneDrive

Downloading and installing OneDrive is a straightforward process, but ensuring that it is set up correctly from the beginning will help you avoid potential challenges later. This section will guide you through the step-by-step process of downloading OneDrive on various platforms, including Windows, macOS, and mobile devices, and offer tips for troubleshooting common installation issues.

1. Overview of the Download Process

OneDrive is available for multiple operating systems, including Windows, macOS, iOS, and Android. It is also pre-installed on most modern Windows operating systems, making the setup even simpler. However, for those using older Windows versions or other operating systems, you may need to download it manually. Here's a breakdown of the download process for each platform:

2. Downloading OneDrive on Windows

OneDrive comes pre-installed on Windows 10 and Windows 11. However, if it's missing or has been uninstalled, follow these steps:

Step 1: Checking for Pre-installed OneDrive

1. Open the **Start Menu** by clicking the Windows icon.

2. Type "OneDrive" in the search bar.

3. If the OneDrive app appears, it's already installed. You can skip to the next section on logging in.

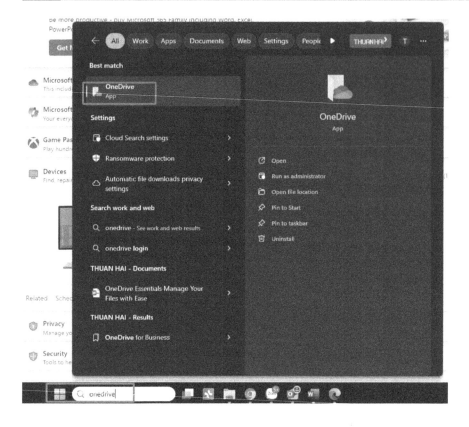

Step 2: Downloading OneDrive Manually

1. Open your web browser and navigate to the <u>Microsoft OneDrive website</u>. / https://www.microsoft.com/onedrive

2. Click the **Download** button prominently displayed on the homepage.

3. Save the installer file to your desired location on your computer.

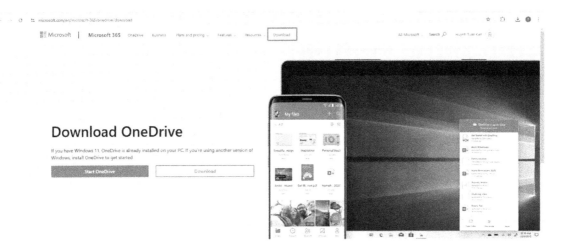

Download the OneDrive mobile app*

Step 3: Installing OneDrive on Windows

1. Locate the downloaded installer file (usually in your "Downloads" folder).

2. Double-click the file to start the installation process.

3. Follow the on-screen prompts:

    o Accept the terms and conditions.

    o Choose whether OneDrive will start automatically when your computer boots.

4. Once installed, OneDrive will appear in the system tray as a cloud icon.

3. Downloading OneDrive on macOS

OneDrive is not pre-installed on macOS, but you can easily download and set it up:

Step 1: Downloading OneDrive

1. Open the **App Store** on your Mac.

2. Search for "OneDrive" in the search bar.

3. Locate the official app published by Microsoft and click **Get** or **Download**.

Alternatively, you can download the app directly from the Microsoft OneDrive website:

1. Navigate to the website in your browser.

2. Select the macOS version and download the installer file.

Step 2: Installing OneDrive on macOS

1. Once the download is complete, locate the installer file (usually in your "Downloads" folder).

2. Double-click the installer to open it.

3. Drag the OneDrive icon into the **Applications** folder.

4. Open the Applications folder and double-click OneDrive to launch the app.

5. Follow the on-screen instructions to log in and complete the setup.

---

4. Downloading OneDrive on Mobile Devices

OneDrive mobile apps allow you to manage your files on the go. The process is similar for both iOS and Android devices:

Step 1: Downloading the App

1. Open your device's app store:

   o   For iOS: Open the **App Store**.

   o   For Android: Open the **Google Play Store**.

2. Search for "Microsoft OneDrive."

3. Locate the official app published by Microsoft Corporation.

4. Tap **Download** or **Install** and wait for the installation to complete.

Step 2: Setting Up OneDrive on Mobile

1. Once the app is installed, tap the OneDrive icon to open it.

2. Sign in using your Microsoft account credentials.

3. Grant the app permissions to access your photos, files, and notifications (if prompted).

4. Customize settings such as **Camera Upload** to automatically back up your photos.

5. Tips for a Smooth Installation Process

While downloading and installing OneDrive is generally seamless, there are a few tips and best practices to ensure a hassle-free experience:

Ensuring System Compatibility

- **Windows**: Ensure your system meets the minimum requirements for OneDrive. For older versions like Windows 7 or 8, a manual download may be required.

- **macOS**: Make sure you are running macOS 10.12 or later for compatibility.

- **Mobile**: Check that your device has the latest operating system updates to support the OneDrive app.

Stable Internet Connection

A stable and fast internet connection is essential for downloading the OneDrive installer and syncing files after installation.

Updating System Software

Before installing OneDrive, update your operating system to the latest version to avoid compatibility issues.

Resolving Installation Errors

If you encounter an error during installation:

1. Restart your device and try again.

2. Ensure that no other Microsoft services are interfering with the installation process.

3. Visit the <u>OneDrive Support Page</u> for troubleshooting guides.

6. Post-Installation Setup

Once OneDrive is installed, follow these steps to ensure everything is set up correctly:

Linking Your Microsoft Account

1. Open the OneDrive app.

2. Enter your Microsoft account email and password.

3. Complete any two-factor authentication steps if enabled.

Configuring Sync Folders

1. Select which folders you want to sync to your device during the initial setup.

2. Choose whether to sync everything or specific folders only.

Exploring the OneDrive Icon

*   On Windows and macOS, a cloud icon will appear in the system tray or menu bar.

*   Right-click this icon to access settings, pause syncing, or open the OneDrive folder.

7. Final Notes on Installation

Congratulations! You've successfully downloaded and installed OneDrive. By following these steps, you now have access to a powerful cloud storage tool that seamlessly integrates with your workflow, no matter which device or operating system you're using. Up next, we'll explore the OneDrive interface and learn how to navigate its various features.

1.1.3 Logging In and Initial Setup

Once you have successfully downloaded and installed OneDrive on your device, the next step is to log in to your account and complete the initial setup. This process ensures that your OneDrive is ready to use, personalized to your needs, and configured for seamless file management. Below, we'll walk you through each stage of logging in and setting up OneDrive for the first time.

1. Logging In to Your OneDrive Account

Step 1: Open the OneDrive Application

- On **Windows**, OneDrive is typically pre-installed as part of the Microsoft Office suite or Windows operating system. You can find it by typing "OneDrive" into the search bar in the Start menu.

- On **Mac**, after installation, the OneDrive app should appear in your Applications folder or Dock.

- For **mobile devices**, locate and open the app from your installed applications list.

Step 2: Enter Your Microsoft Account Credentials

- When you open the app for the first time, a login screen will appear prompting you to enter your Microsoft account credentials.

  - If you already have an account, type in your **email address or phone number** associated with your Microsoft account, then click **Next**.

  - If you do not have an account, go back to **1.1.1 Creating a Microsoft Account** and follow the steps to create one before returning to log in.

Step 3: Enter Your Password

- After entering your email, the system will request your account password.

  - Ensure you enter the password correctly, keeping in mind capitalization and any special characters.

  - If you've forgotten your password, click on the **Forgot Password** link to reset it via your email or phone number.

Step 4: Enable Two-Factor Authentication (Optional)

- If your account has two-factor authentication enabled, you will receive a verification code via text message, email, or an authenticator app. Enter this code to verify your identity.

  - This step provides an added layer of security, especially for protecting sensitive files stored in OneDrive.

2. Initial Setup Process

After successfully logging in, OneDrive will guide you through a short setup process. This step ensures that your files are synced correctly, and that the application is configured to suit your preferences.

Step 1: Choosing Folders to Sync

- OneDrive will prompt you to select folders from your computer to sync with your OneDrive cloud storage.

  o You can choose to sync all files and folders or select specific ones. For example, you might sync your Documents, Pictures, and Desktop folders.

  o Click on **Sync Options** or **Choose Folders** to customize this selection.

Tip: If you're using OneDrive for work or school, prioritize syncing project folders or shared workspaces that you access frequently.

Step 2: Configuring Sync Settings

- After selecting the folders, you will see options to configure how and when files are synced:

  o **Always keep files on this device:** Ensures a local copy of your files is available even without an internet connection.

  o **On-demand sync:** Files are downloaded only when accessed, saving storage space on your device.

Recommendation: Use on-demand sync if you have limited storage on your device but still want access to your full file library in the cloud.

Step 3: Setting Up File Backup

- OneDrive allows you to back up important files automatically. The system will prompt you to back up your Desktop, Documents, and Pictures folders to the cloud.

  o Click **Start Backup** to enable this feature.

  o If you prefer not to back up certain folders, deselect them in this step.

Step 4: Select Default Save Locations

- During setup, you can choose whether OneDrive will be your default save location for new files.

  o Selecting this option ensures that any new files you create in Office apps (e.g., Word, Excel) are automatically saved to your OneDrive folder.

  o If you prefer local storage, you can opt out of this feature and manually upload files to OneDrive later.

3. Personalizing Your OneDrive Experience

Once the basic setup is complete, OneDrive provides options to personalize the experience further. These steps ensure that the platform aligns with your workflow and preferences.

Step 1: Choosing Themes and Appearance

- OneDrive's interface offers both **light mode** and **dark mode** options.

  o Dark mode is ideal for reducing eye strain in low-light environments.

  o You can toggle this setting in the app's settings menu under **Appearance**.

Step 2: Notifications and Alerts

- Customize your notifications to stay informed about file changes, sharing activities, and syncing issues.

  o For example, enable alerts for when someone edits a shared file or when a file fails to sync.

- o   Adjust these settings under **Preferences > Notifications**.

Step 3: Language and Regional Settings

- If you work in multiple languages or regions, OneDrive allows you to select your preferred language and time zone.

    - o   Go to **Account Settings** to configure these options.

---

4. Exploring the OneDrive Folder on Your Device

After completing the setup, OneDrive will create a dedicated folder on your computer or mobile device. This folder acts as the central hub for your synced files.

Step 1: Locating the OneDrive Folder

- On Windows, the OneDrive folder is typically located under **This PC** in File Explorer.

- On Mac, you can find it in Finder under **Favorites**.

- For mobile devices, the app's home screen serves as your OneDrive folder.

Step 2: Understanding Folder Icons

- Different icons in the OneDrive folder provide important information about your files:

    - o   **Cloud icon:** The file is stored online only.

    - o   **Green checkmark icon:** The file is downloaded and available offline.

    - o   **Red X icon:** There is an issue with syncing the file.

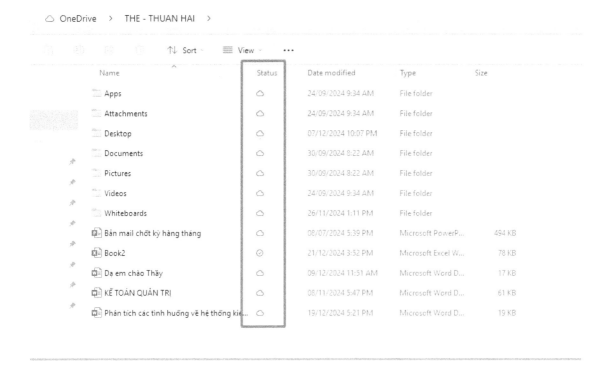

5. Testing Your Setup

To ensure everything is working correctly, perform a quick test:

1. Create a new folder in your OneDrive folder and name it **Test Folder**.

2. Upload a file, such as a photo or document, to this folder.

3. Access the file from another device using the OneDrive app or web version to confirm it has synced properly.

6. Troubleshooting Login and Setup Issues

If you encounter issues during login or setup, here are some common problems and solutions:

- **Problem:** Cannot log in due to incorrect credentials.

  o **Solution:** Double-check your email and password, and reset your password if needed.

- **Problem:** Syncing is not working after setup.

  o **Solution:** Ensure your internet connection is stable, and restart the app.

By completing the login and initial setup, you are now ready to take full advantage of OneDrive's powerful features. Next, we'll explore the OneDrive interface in detail to help you navigate and manage your files effectively.

1.2 Exploring the OneDrive Interface

1.2.1 Desktop Application Overview

The OneDrive desktop application is a powerful tool designed to seamlessly integrate cloud storage into your computer's file system. By understanding its features, layout, and functions, you can maximize productivity and make file management a breeze. This section offers a detailed breakdown of the desktop application interface, from initial setup to advanced functionality.

Getting Acquainted with the OneDrive Icon

Once the OneDrive desktop application is installed and configured, its presence is signified by the **OneDrive icon** in the taskbar or menu bar, depending on your operating system. This small cloud-shaped icon is your primary point of interaction with OneDrive on the desktop.

1. **The Icon's Color Indicators**:

    o   **Blue Cloud**: Indicates that OneDrive is working properly, and all files are up-to-date in the cloud.

    o   **Gray Cloud**: Suggests the account is signed out or not yet connected.

    o   **Green Checkmark (Solid)**: Files or folders are stored locally on the device and are synced with OneDrive.

- o **Red Cross**: Highlights a sync issue that requires immediate attention.

2. **Accessing the OneDrive Menu**:

   - o Clicking on the OneDrive icon opens a small menu, giving you access to key features:

     - **File Sync Status**: A visual representation of ongoing and completed syncs.

     - **Settings Gear**: Provides options to manage accounts, change preferences, and troubleshoot.

     - **Help and Feedback**: Direct links for support resources and submitting feedback.

     - **Pause Syncing**: An option to temporarily halt syncing activities when bandwidth conservation is needed.

Navigating the File Explorer/ Finder Integration

OneDrive integrates directly with your operating system's native file manager, such as **File Explorer** on Windows or **Finder** on macOS. This integration creates a dedicated OneDrive folder, providing a seamless experience for managing your files.

1. **The OneDrive Folder**:

   - o The OneDrive folder is automatically created during setup and is prominently displayed in the file manager's sidebar. It serves as a gateway to all files stored in the cloud.

   - o You can organize the folder by creating subfolders, moving files, and renaming items just as you would with local files.

2. **Sync Status Icons**:

   - o Each file and folder has a small icon that indicates its sync status:

- **Cloud Icon**: The file exists only in the cloud and doesn't consume local storage.

- **Green Checkmark**: The file is downloaded and available offline.

- **Blue Arrows**: The file is actively syncing.

  o These icons provide real-time updates, helping you manage file availability and storage efficiently.

3. **Context Menu Options**:

  o Right-clicking a file or folder in the OneDrive folder reveals additional options:

    - **Always Keep on This Device**: Ensures the file is permanently available offline.

    - **Free Up Space**: Removes the local copy while keeping it in the cloud.

    - **View Online**: Opens the file directly in the OneDrive web interface.

    - **Share**: Allows you to generate shareable links or set permissions directly from the desktop.

Accessing and Managing Multiple Accounts

OneDrive desktop supports multiple accounts, making it an excellent choice for users who need to separate personal and work files. To switch between accounts or add a new one:

1. **Adding an Account**:

  o Open the OneDrive menu from the taskbar.

  o Click on the **Settings Gear** and navigate to the **Account** tab.

  o Select **Add an Account**, and follow the setup process by entering the credentials for the new account.

2. **Switching Between Accounts**:

   o Both accounts will appear as separate folders in File Explorer or Finder.

   o Each account has its own sync preferences, ensuring clear segregation of files.

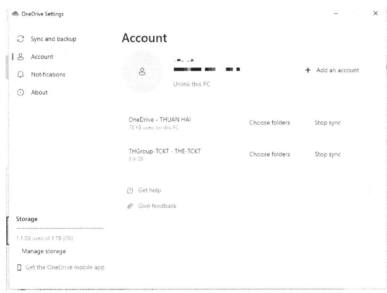

Customizing Sync Preferences

OneDrive offers the flexibility to sync only specific files or folders to your local device, optimizing both storage and bandwidth. Customizing sync preferences is an essential skill for managing your storage efficiently.

1. **Selective Sync**:

   o   Open the OneDrive menu and go to **Settings > Account > Choose Folders**.

   o   Uncheck any folders you don't need locally. These will remain available in the cloud but won't occupy local space.

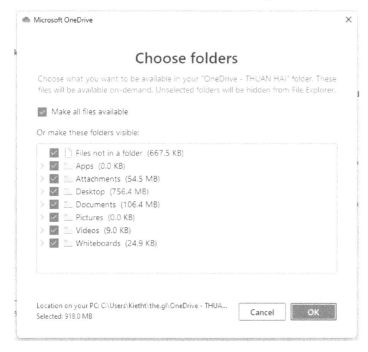

2. **Adjusting Bandwidth Settings**:

   o   If you're concerned about network usage, OneDrive allows you to limit upload and download speeds.

   o   Navigate to **Settings > Network** and set bandwidth limits based on your requirements.

Understanding Advanced Settings

The desktop application provides various advanced settings to give you more control over your OneDrive experience:

1. **Backup Options**:

   o OneDrive can automatically back up key folders such as Desktop, Documents, and Pictures. This feature ensures critical files are protected without requiring manual uploads.

   o To enable, go to **Settings > Backup > Manage Backup**, and select the folders you want to include.

2. **Notification Settings**:

   o Stay informed about sync status, shared file activity, or account changes by enabling notifications in the **Settings > Notifications** menu.

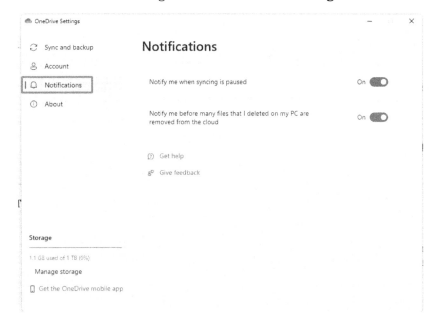

3. **Troubleshooting Tools**:

   o For resolving sync issues or other technical glitches, the **Help & Settings** section includes tools to reset the application or view logs.

Tips for Maximizing Productivity with the Desktop App

1. **Keyboard Shortcuts**:

   o Quickly access OneDrive features with handy shortcuts, such as pressing **Win + E** to open File Explorer or **Command + Shift + O** on macOS to open Finder.

2. **Pinning Folders to Quick Access**:

   o Frequently used folders can be pinned to the Quick Access section in File Explorer or Finder for even faster navigation.

3. **Using Offline Mode Strategically**:

   o Download large project folders ahead of time when traveling or working in areas with limited internet access.

Conclusion

The desktop application serves as a bridge between your local file system and the cloud, ensuring that your files are always accessible, secure, and synchronized. By mastering the features outlined above, you can confidently organize, manage, and collaborate on your OneDrive files without ever leaving your desktop environment. With its intuitive interface and robust integration, OneDrive empowers you to stay productive wherever you are.

1.2.2 Web Version Features

OneDrive's web version offers a versatile, user-friendly experience that allows you to access, manage, and share your files from anywhere, provided you have an internet connection. This section provides an in-depth walkthrough of the features of the OneDrive web interface, helping you get familiar with its tools and capabilities.

Overview of the OneDrive Web Interface

Upon logging in to the OneDrive web version through a browser at onedrive.live.com, you'll land on the **Home Screen**. This interface is designed to give you quick access to your files, organize content, and collaborate efficiently. Key areas of the interface include:

1. **Navigation Pane** (Left Side)

2. **Main Content Area** (Center)

3. **Toolbar and Command Options** (Top)

4. **Account Settings and Notifications** (Top-Right Corner)

Let's dive into each section in detail to understand how you can use the web version to its full potential.

1. Navigation Pane

The **Navigation Pane** on the left side of the interface is the central hub for accessing your files, folders, and shared content. It contains several key sections:

1.1 My Files

This is the main section where all your uploaded and synced files reside. It acts as your personal cloud storage folder. Within "My Files," you can:

- Browse through folders and files in a directory view.

- Sort files by name, date modified, size, or type.

- Use folder structures to organize your files systematically.

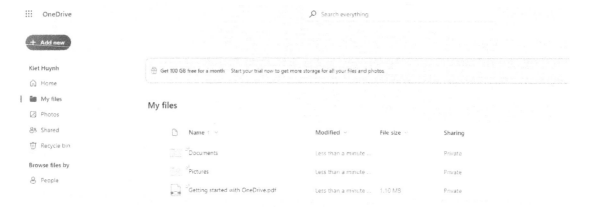

1.2 Recent

The "Recent" section lists files that you've recently opened, edited, or interacted with. It provides quick access to the content you're actively working on.

- Files are displayed in a chronological order, with the most recent at the top.

- This feature saves time by eliminating the need to search through folders manually.

1.3 Photos

The "Photos" section automatically organizes all image files stored in your OneDrive. It uses AI to group your photos based on tags and dates. Key features include:

- **Automatic Albums**: OneDrive creates albums for specific events or days.

- **Filtering Options**: You can filter photos by tags, date, and location metadata.

- **Photo Viewer**: Clicking on a photo opens a viewer where you can zoom, rotate, or share it directly.

1.4 Shared

The "Shared" section displays all files and folders that have been shared with you, as well as content you've shared with others. This section helps you:

- Keep track of collaborations and shared documents.

- View who has access to shared files and folders.

- Manage permissions, such as editing or revoking access.

1.5 Recycle Bin

Deleted files and folders are stored in the **Recycle Bin** for up to 30 days (or 93 days for business plans). From here, you can:

- **Restore Files**: Recover accidentally deleted files to their original location.

- **Permanently Delete Files**: Free up storage space by permanently deleting files.

1.6 Storage Metrics

At the bottom of the Navigation Pane, you'll find a summary of your OneDrive storage usage. This shows:

- Total storage space available.

- Storage used so far.

- Options to upgrade your storage plan.

2. Main Content Area

The **Main Content Area** in the center of the screen dynamically changes based on the section you are viewing. It displays folders, files, and related tools. Let's explore its functionality:

2.1 File and Folder View

Your content is displayed in either a **List View** or a **Tile View**:

- **List View**: Shows files and folders in rows, along with details like file type, size, and date modified.

- **Tile View**: Displays larger file icons for easier visual identification.

You can toggle between these views using the icons in the top-right corner of the Main Content Area.

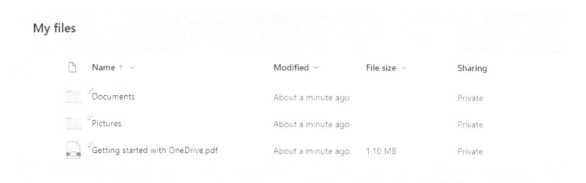

2.2 File Commands

When you select a file or folder, a **Command Bar** appears at the top of the Main Content Area. Key actions include:

- **Open**: View files directly in the browser or open them in Microsoft Office Online.

- **Download**: Save a copy of the file or folder to your local device.

- **Share**: Generate a link to share content with others or invite specific people.

- **Delete**: Move items to the Recycle Bin.

- **Move/Copy**: Organize files by moving them to a different folder.

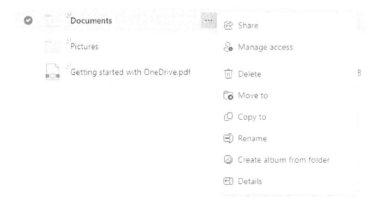

2.3 File Previews

OneDrive's web interface allows you to preview most file types without downloading them. Supported file formats include:

- Documents (Word, Excel, PowerPoint, PDFs)

- Images (JPG, PNG, GIF, BMP)

- Videos (MP4, AVI, MOV)

- Audio files (MP3, WAV)

Simply click on a file, and a preview pane opens. You can scroll through multi-page documents or play media files directly within OneDrive.

3. Toolbar and Command Options

The **Toolbar** at the top of the screen contains quick-access buttons to streamline file management. These include:

3.1 Upload Button

The **Upload** button allows you to add files or folders to your OneDrive. You can:

- **Upload Files**: Add individual files directly from your device.

- **Upload Folders**: Add an entire folder and its contents in one go.

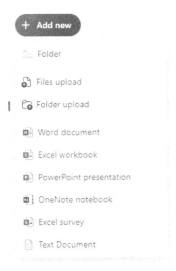

3.2 New Button

The **New** button lets you create new items within your OneDrive. Options include:

- **Folders**: Organize your files by creating a new folder.

- **Office Files**: Create Word, Excel, PowerPoint, or OneNote documents directly in OneDrive.

3.3 Sort and Filter

You can sort and filter files using the toolbar. Options include:

- **Sort By**: Name, Modified Date, File Size, or Type.

- **Filter**: Narrow results based on keywords, file types, or dates.

3.4 Search Bar

The **Search Bar**, located at the top of the toolbar, is a powerful tool for locating files. It searches filenames, file contents, and metadata, ensuring you find what you need quickly.

---

4. Account Settings and Notifications

In the top-right corner, you'll find the **Account Menu** and **Notifications** icons.

4.1 Account Menu

Clicking your profile picture or initials gives you access to:

- **Personal Settings**: Change your name, profile picture, or email preferences.

- **Storage Details**: Check your current usage and upgrade plans.

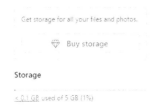

- **Sign Out**: Log out of your OneDrive account.

4.2 Notifications

The **Notifications Icon** provides alerts about:

- Shared file updates (e.g., someone edited a document).

- Storage limits or warnings.

- Sync issues that require attention.

Conclusion

The OneDrive web version offers a clean, intuitive interface that simplifies file management. By mastering the Navigation Pane, Main Content Area, and Toolbar features, you can efficiently organize, access, and collaborate on your files from any device. Whether you're uploading documents, sharing content, or previewing files, OneDrive's web interface ensures you have everything you need at your fingertips.

1.2.3 Mobile App Navigation

Introduction to OneDrive Mobile App

OneDrive's mobile application brings the power of cloud storage to your fingertips, offering seamless access to your files and folders anytime, anywhere. Whether you're using a smartphone or tablet, the app allows you to manage your digital assets efficiently while staying connected on the go. Designed for both **iOS** and **Android**, the OneDrive mobile app is intuitive and feature-rich, making it easy for users to upload, view, organize, and share files.

This section will guide you step-by-step through the layout, features, and functionalities of the OneDrive mobile app so that you can navigate it with confidence.

Installing and Setting Up the OneDrive Mobile App

Before diving into the navigation, ensure the OneDrive app is installed and ready to use on your device.

1. **Downloading the App**:

    o   For iOS devices, visit the Apple App Store.

    o   For Android devices, access the Google Play Store.

    o   Search for "OneDrive," then download and install the app.

2. **Signing In**:

    o   Open the app after installation.

    o   Log in using your Microsoft account credentials. If you don't have an account, tap **"Sign Up"** to create one.

    o   Once logged in, you'll see the main interface, which we will explore in detail next.

Overview of the Main Navigation Elements

The OneDrive mobile app has a clean and organized layout. Let's break down each key area of the interface to understand its purpose.

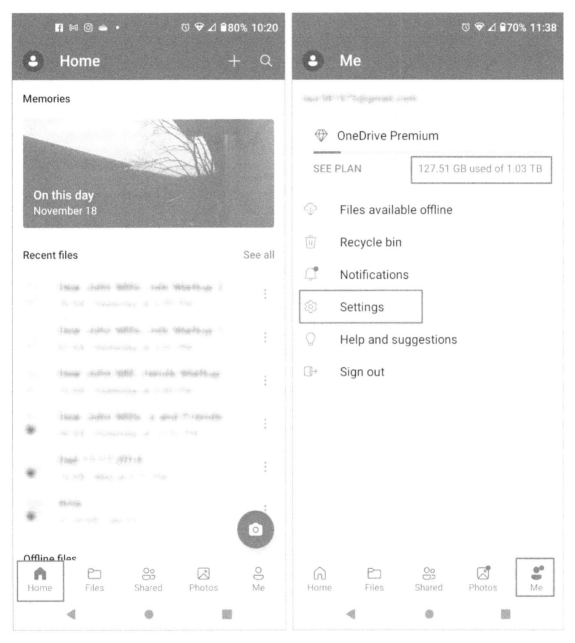

1. **Bottom Navigation Bar**

The bottom navigation bar is the central hub of the app, providing quick access to essential features:

- o **Files Tab**: View all your files and folders stored in OneDrive. This is the default landing page when you open the app.

- o **Recent Tab**: Quickly access files you've recently opened, edited, or added.

- o **Shared Tab**: View files and folders that others have shared with you or that you have shared with others.

- o **Photos Tab**: Browse all photos and videos uploaded to your OneDrive. The app automatically organizes photos by date.

- o **Me Tab**: Access account settings, manage your storage, and view offline files.

2. **Top Navigation Bar**

At the top of the app, you'll find tools and options to streamline your experience:

- o **Search Icon**: Use the search bar to find files, folders, or photos quickly. You can search by keywords, file types, or even specific file names.

- o **Camera Icon**: Instantly upload photos or documents by taking a picture. Ideal for digitizing receipts, forms, or whiteboard notes.

- o **+ Add Icon**: Tap the "+" button to add new items to OneDrive, such as:

  - ▪ Upload a file or folder

  - ▪ Create a new folder

  - ▪ Scan a document

  - ▪ Take a photo and save it directly to OneDrive

Navigating the Files Tab

The **Files** tab serves as the backbone of the app, where you can browse, manage, and organize your stored items. Here's how to make the most of it:

1. **Viewing Your Files and Folders**

- o Tap on any folder to open it and view its contents.

- o Use swipe gestures to scroll through long lists of files.

o File icons indicate different file types (e.g., documents, images, videos).

2. **Organizing Files**

   o **Creating Folders**: Tap the "+" icon > **"Create Folder"**. Name the folder and confirm.

   o **Renaming Files**: Press and hold on a file > select **"Rename"** from the menu.

   o **Moving Files**: Tap and hold a file > **"Move"**, then choose the destination folder.

3. **File Previews**

   o Tap on a file to preview it without downloading it fully. The app supports previews for documents (Word, Excel, PowerPoint), PDFs, photos, and videos.

4. **File Options Menu**

   o Tap the **three dots** (⋮) next to any file to reveal options:

      ▪ Share

      ▪ Move

      ▪ Copy

      ▪ Delete

      ▪ Download for offline access

Using the Recent and Shared Tabs

1. **Recent Tab**

   The **Recent** tab displays a chronological list of files you've recently interacted with, allowing quick access to frequently used documents. You can:

   o Tap a file to open it.

   o Swipe left or right to navigate between files.

2. **Shared Tab**

- o View all shared files under **"Shared with you"** and **"Shared by you"** sections.

- o Tap on a shared file to preview it or edit it (depending on permissions).

- o Manage shared content by adjusting permissions, copying the file, or removing access.

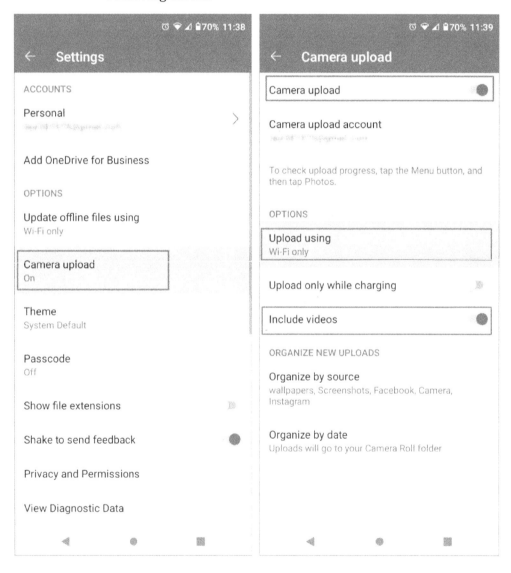

Photos Tab: Managing Your Images and Videos

The **Photos** tab offers a visual way to browse all images and videos stored on OneDrive.

1. **Photo Organization**

   o The app automatically groups photos by date (e.g., "This Month," "Last Month").

   o Use the search bar to locate specific images using keywords, such as "beach" or "documents."

2. **Camera Upload**

   o Enable **Camera Upload** to automatically back up photos and videos from your mobile device to OneDrive.

      ▪ Go to **Me Tab** > **Settings** > **Camera Upload**.

      ▪ Customize settings to include videos and choose upload quality.

3. **Photo Actions**

   o Tap on a photo to view it in full screen. From here, you can:

      ▪ Download

      ▪ Share

      ▪ Edit (basic cropping, rotation, and filters)

      ▪ Delete

Me Tab: Managing Your Account and Settings

The **Me** tab provides access to account settings, storage information, and offline files.

1. **Account Settings**

   o View your account details (email, plan type, and storage usage).

   o Upgrade to a higher OneDrive plan if needed.

2. **Offline Files**

- View files you've marked for offline access, allowing you to use them without an internet connection.

3. **App Settings**

- Customize OneDrive preferences, such as:

    - Enable **Camera Upload**

    - Set **Notification Preferences**

    - Adjust **File Download Quality**

Scanning and Uploading Documents

One of the standout features of the OneDrive mobile app is its built-in document scanning tool.

1. **Scanning a Document**

- Tap the **"+" icon** > **"Scan"**.

- Use your camera to scan physical documents (receipts, contracts, notes).

- Adjust the scan area and confirm.

2. **Enhancing Scans**

- After scanning, you can enhance the document by adjusting brightness, cropping, or applying filters.

3. **Saving Scans**

- Save the scanned document as a PDF or image directly to a specified OneDrive folder.

Conclusion

The OneDrive mobile app provides robust functionality that enables you to manage your files seamlessly while on the move. By understanding the navigation elements and key features, you can organize, share, and access your files with ease. Whether you're backing up photos, scanning documents, or collaborating on files, the mobile app ensures your data is always at your fingertips.

Next, we will explore **"1.3 Understanding OneDrive Plans"**, where you'll learn about subscription options tailored to your needs.

1.3 Understanding OneDrive Plans

1.3.1 Free vs. Paid Subscriptions

When starting with OneDrive, it is essential to understand the different plans Microsoft offers. These plans vary in features, pricing, and storage limits, allowing users to choose the option that best fits their needs. Whether you are an individual, a student, or a business professional, Microsoft provides a tailored solution for everyone. In this section, we will examine the **Free** and **Paid subscriptions**, compare their features, and help you determine which plan aligns with your personal or professional requirements.

The Free OneDrive Plan

The Free OneDrive plan is perfect for individuals or casual users who only require basic cloud storage capabilities. It is Microsoft's entry-level offering and comes with a **free allocation of 5 GB of storage**. This plan is widely accessible, requiring only a Microsoft account to get started.

Key Features of the Free Plan

1. **5 GB of Cloud Storage**

   o The 5 GB storage allows you to store essential files, such as documents, photos, and small videos. It is sufficient for lightweight usage, such as backing up school assignments, storing resumes, or syncing personal files across devices.

   o Compared to other free cloud services like Google Drive (15 GB) or iCloud (5 GB), OneDrive holds a competitive position, especially for users already integrated into the Microsoft ecosystem.

2. **Sync Across Devices**

   o The Free plan allows users to synchronize files across their devices, including PCs, smartphones, and tablets. Whether you are using Windows, Mac, iOS, or Android, the OneDrive app ensures that your data is accessible from anywhere.

o Changes made to files on one device will reflect across all synced devices almost instantaneously.

3. **Web and Mobile Access**

   o Users can access their OneDrive files from the **OneDrive website** or the mobile app. This provides flexibility for those on the go, allowing them to upload, download, or share files easily.

   o The mobile app supports features like camera upload, enabling automatic backups of your photos and videos directly to OneDrive.

4. **Basic Sharing Options**

   o The Free plan enables basic file sharing with friends, family, or colleagues. You can share files and folders through shareable links, granting permissions to view, edit, or download the content.

   o This feature is particularly useful for personal collaboration, such as sharing vacation photos, group projects, or event planning documents.

5. **Integration with Microsoft Office Online**

   o OneDrive's Free plan allows seamless access to **Microsoft Office Online** tools like Word, Excel, PowerPoint, and OneNote. Users can create and edit documents in these applications without needing a paid Office subscription.

   o This is a significant advantage for students and professionals who need access to Office tools without incurring additional costs.

Who Should Use the Free Plan?

The Free OneDrive plan is ideal for:

- **Students** who need basic cloud storage to back up school projects and assignments.

- **Casual Users** who want to store a small collection of files, such as personal photos, videos, and important documents.

- **Individuals on a Budget** who do not require advanced storage or collaboration tools.

While the Free plan is a fantastic starting point, it does have limitations. Users who need more storage, enhanced collaboration features, or security upgrades may find the paid plans more suitable.

Paid OneDrive Subscriptions

Microsoft offers several paid OneDrive plans under two primary categories: **OneDrive Standalone Plans** and **Microsoft 365 Subscriptions**. These paid options unlock additional storage, advanced features, and integrations tailored for individuals, families, and businesses.

OneDrive Standalone Plans

The standalone plans are focused solely on providing additional cloud storage without the added cost of Microsoft 365 services. These options are perfect for users who only need more space and do not require access to Microsoft Office tools.

1. **OneDrive Standalone 100 GB Plan**

    o   **Cost**: Approximately $1.99 per month.

    o   **Storage**: Provides 100 GB of cloud storage.

    o   This plan is designed for individuals who need extra space for documents, photos, and small videos but do not require a full Microsoft 365 subscription.

    o   It includes all the features of the Free plan, such as file syncing, basic sharing, and access to the OneDrive mobile app.

2. **Who Should Use the 100 GB Plan?**

    o   **Photographers and Creators** who need extra space to back up media files.

    o   **Students and Professionals** who work with large documents, presentations, and spreadsheets.

    o   **Individuals with Growing Storage Needs** who have outgrown the 5 GB free allocation.

Microsoft 365 Subscriptions

For users who want the best value and access to advanced tools, Microsoft offers OneDrive as part of the **Microsoft 365 subscription plans**. These subscriptions not only include expanded OneDrive storage but also come bundled with powerful Office applications, security features, and collaboration tools.

1. **Microsoft 365 Personal**

   o **Cost**: Approximately $6.99 per month or $69.99 annually.

   o **Storage**: Includes 1 TB of OneDrive storage (1,000 GB).

   o **Features**:

       ▪ Full access to premium versions of Microsoft Word, Excel, PowerPoint, and Outlook.

       ▪ Ransomware protection and advanced security options.

       ▪ The ability to use Microsoft Office apps on up to 5 devices simultaneously.

   o This plan is tailored for individual users who need extensive storage and professional tools.

2. **Microsoft 365 Family**

   o **Cost**: Approximately $9.99 per month or $99.99 annually.

   o **Storage**: Includes up to **6 TB of storage** (1 TB per user for up to 6 users).

   o **Features**:

       ▪ All the features of the Microsoft 365 Personal plan.

       ▪ Family Safety tools for managing screen time and app usage.

   o This plan is ideal for families who want shared access to storage and Office tools at an affordable price.

Benefits of Paid Subscriptions

1. **Massive Storage**

- o Paid plans offer significantly more storage, with up to 1 TB per user. This is perfect for storing large files, such as high-resolution videos, extensive photo libraries, and project backups.

2. **Advanced Security**

- o Features like **Personal Vault**, ransomware detection, and file recovery provide enhanced protection for your sensitive data.

3. **Offline Access and Premium Sync**

- o Paid plans allow you to sync large folders seamlessly and enable offline access to files with full editing capabilities.

4. **Seamless Integration with Microsoft Ecosystem**

- o Access to premium Microsoft Office tools enhances productivity, collaboration, and workflow management.

Free vs. Paid Subscriptions: A Quick Comparison

Free vs. Paid OneDrive Subscriptions: Full Comparison

Feature	Free Plan	OneDrive 100 GB Plan	Microsoft 365 Personal	Microsoft 365 Family
Monthly Cost	Free	$1.99/month	$6.99/month or $69.99/year	$9.99/month or $99.99/year
Storage Limit	5 GB	100 GB	1 TB (1,000 GB)	1 TB per user (up to 6 TB total)
Number of Users	1 User	1 User	1 User	Up to 6 Users
File Sync Across Devices	Yes	Yes	Yes	Yes
Access on Web and Mobile	Yes	Yes	Yes	Yes
File Sharing	Basic Sharing	Basic Sharing	Advanced Sharing with Permissions	Advanced Sharing with Permissions
Access to Office Apps	Online Office Apps Only	Not Included	Full Premium Office Apps (Desktop, Web, Mobile)	Full Premium Office Apps (Desktop, Web, Mobile)

Collaboration Features	Limited (Web Only)	Limited (Storage Only)	Real-Time Co-Authoring	Real-Time Co-Authoring
Personal Vault	Limited (3 Files)	Not Included	Included with Advanced Security	Included with Advanced Security
Ransomware Protection	Not Included	Not Included	Included (File Recovery up to 30 Days)	Included (File Recovery up to 30 Days)
Advanced Security Features	No	No	Yes (Password-Protected Sharing, Encrypted Files)	Yes (Password-Protected Sharing, Encrypted Files)
Automatic Backup (Photos/Files)	Yes (Manual Setup)	Yes	Yes	Yes
Family Safety Features	No	No	No	Yes (Parental Controls, Location Sharing)
Support	Basic Support	Basic Support	Priority Customer Support	Priority Customer Support

Key Notes:

1. **Free Plan**: Ideal for casual users needing basic cloud storage and file syncing.

2. **100 GB Plan**: Suitable for individuals requiring extra storage without Office apps.

3. **Microsoft 365 Personal**: Great for individuals seeking full-featured cloud storage (1 TB) and premium Office applications.

4. **Microsoft 365 Family**: Best value for families, offering up to 6 TB of storage (1 TB per user) and additional tools like Family Safety.

Conclusion

Choosing between the **Free** and **Paid subscriptions** ultimately depends on your specific needs. For casual users, the Free plan may be sufficient for light storage and basic tasks.

However, for professionals, students, or families who need additional storage, advanced tools, and enhanced security, upgrading to a paid OneDrive plan—especially as part of Microsoft 365—offers unparalleled value and convenience.

In the next section, we will dive deeper into **Business and Enterprise Options**, exploring how OneDrive can meet the needs of companies, large and small.

1.3.2 Business and Enterprise Options

When using OneDrive for business purposes, you'll find that Microsoft offers more advanced and robust plans designed to meet the needs of organizations, whether small businesses or large enterprises. In this section, we'll break down the specific features, pricing structures, and benefits of the **Business** and **Enterprise** versions of OneDrive. This will help you determine which option is the best fit for your team or company.

1. Overview of OneDrive for Business

OneDrive for Business is part of the Microsoft 365 suite, specifically tailored for organizations to improve file storage, collaboration, and overall productivity. Unlike the personal version of OneDrive, the business plans offer enhanced features like centralized administration, security tools, and compliance capabilities.

OneDrive for Business is available as part of several Microsoft 365 subscriptions or as a standalone product. Businesses can integrate OneDrive with other Microsoft tools like SharePoint, Teams, and Outlook to streamline workflows.

The key differentiator in OneDrive Business plans is that data ownership lies with the organization instead of the individual user. This gives IT administrators greater control over user accounts, storage, permissions, and security settings.

2. OneDrive Business Plans: Features and Pricing

Microsoft offers **two primary types of business plans**:

1. **OneDrive for Business Plan 1**

2. **OneDrive for Business Plan 2**

Below is a detailed breakdown of each plan.

2.1 OneDrive for Business Plan 1

This plan is ideal for small to medium-sized businesses that need basic file storage and sharing capabilities without additional advanced compliance features. It focuses on core OneDrive functionality.

Key Features:

- **Storage Capacity:** 1 TB per user.

- **File Upload Limit:** Supports file uploads up to **250 GB** in size.

- **Secure File Sharing:** Share files both internally and externally with password protection and link expiration.

- **Access Across Devices:** Access files through desktop, web, and mobile applications.

- **File Sync:** Sync files to your device and work offline. Changes are automatically updated when you reconnect to the internet.

- **Version History:** Retrieve previous versions of files for up to **30 days**.

- **Integration with Office Online:** Edit Word, Excel, PowerPoint, and OneNote files directly in your browser.

- **Basic Security:** Data encryption both **in-transit** and **at-rest**.

Pricing:
As of 2024, OneDrive for Business Plan 1 costs **$5.00 per user/month** (annual subscription).

Who Should Choose This Plan?

- Small businesses or startups that need reliable and secure file storage.

- Teams that collaborate using Office Online and don't require extensive compliance features.

2.2 OneDrive for Business Plan 2

This plan is suited for businesses that require advanced data protection, compliance, and management tools. It includes everything in **Plan 1** but offers more robust features for organizations with complex IT requirements.

Key Features:

- **Unlimited Storage:** Each user receives **1 TB initially**, with the option to expand storage to **unlimited** upon request.

- **Advanced Security Features:**

    - Files are scanned for malware.

    - Enhanced encryption at-rest with **per-file encryption**.

    - Detection of ransomware or unusual activity, with alerts and recovery options.

- **Compliance Tools:**

    - Meet industry compliance standards such as **GDPR**, **HIPAA**, and ISO 27001.

    - Use **eDiscovery** to find, manage, and preserve data across your organization.

- **Data Loss Prevention (DLP):** Protect sensitive data by identifying and preventing unauthorized sharing of confidential files.

- **Version History:** Restore previous versions of files for up to **365 days**.

- **User Management:** Admins have centralized control over user permissions, file access, and security settings.

- **Audit Logs and Reports:** Generate reports to monitor user activity and file access.

Pricing:
OneDrive for Business Plan 2 is priced at **$10.00 per user/month** (annual subscription).

Who Should Choose This Plan?

- Businesses and organizations that deal with sensitive or regulated data.

- Companies that require enhanced security and compliance tools.

- Teams that need access to advanced administrative controls and reports.

3. OneDrive for Enterprise: Features and Benefits

For larger organizations with more demanding needs, Microsoft offers **OneDrive for Enterprise** as part of its Microsoft 365 E1, E3, and E5 plans. These plans include not only OneDrive but also SharePoint, Microsoft Teams, Outlook, and other tools to support enterprise-level collaboration and workflows.

Below is a breakdown of enterprise plan options and their additional capabilities:

3.1 OneDrive as Part of Microsoft 365 Enterprise Plans

Plan	Storage	Key Features	Pricing
Microsoft 365 E1	1 TB per user	File storage, Teams, SharePoint, Office Online, basic DLP.	$10.00 per user/month
Microsoft 365 E3	Unlimited Storage	Includes E1 features + advanced DLP, threat protection, compliance tools.	$23.00 per user/month
Microsoft 365 E5	Unlimited Storage	E3 features + advanced analytics, AI-powered threat detection.	$38.00 per user/month

3.2 Enterprise-Level Features

- **Unlimited Storage:** Perfect for organizations with massive data requirements.

- **Advanced Threat Protection:** Proactive scanning for malicious files and advanced ransomware detection.

- **Compliance and eDiscovery:** Tools to help organizations adhere to legal and industry-specific regulations.

- **AI and Analytics:** Integration of Microsoft's AI tools to provide insights, optimize workflows, and analyze usage patterns.

- **Granular Admin Controls:** Centralized management for security, permissions, and data access across thousands of users.

- **Mobile Device Management (MDM):** Securely manage OneDrive data across company-issued and personal devices.

4. Choosing the Right Plan for Your Organization

When selecting the appropriate OneDrive plan for your business or enterprise, consider the following factors:

1. **Storage Requirements:**

   o   Does your organization need 1 TB per user, or will it require unlimited storage?

2. **Security and Compliance:**

   o   Do you need basic file encryption, or are advanced compliance tools (like GDPR or HIPAA) necessary?

3. **User Count:**

   o   Small teams may find **Plan 1** sufficient, while larger organizations often benefit from **Plan 2** or enterprise plans.

4. **Integration Needs:**

   o   Do you require seamless integration with Microsoft Teams, SharePoint, or other Microsoft 365 tools?

5. Conclusion: Unlocking Business Potential with OneDrive

OneDrive's Business and Enterprise plans offer organizations an efficient, secure, and scalable solution for file storage, sharing, and collaboration. By choosing the right plan, businesses can streamline workflows, improve productivity, and protect sensitive data.

Whether you are a small business aiming to manage files effectively or an enterprise requiring robust compliance and advanced security tools, OneDrive provides solutions to meet your needs. The ability to integrate with Microsoft's ecosystem, along with generous storage options and cutting-edge security features, makes OneDrive a must-have tool for modern businesses.

Take the time to evaluate your organization's specific requirements, and leverage OneDrive to unlock your team's full potential.

CHAPTER II
Uploading and Organizing Files

2.1 Uploading Files and Folders

2.1.1 Drag-and-Drop Uploads

Uploading files and folders to OneDrive using the drag-and-drop method is one of the simplest and most intuitive ways to add content to your cloud storage. This method allows you to seamlessly transfer files from your computer to OneDrive without the need to click multiple buttons or navigate through menus. By simply selecting your desired file(s) or folder(s), dragging them to the OneDrive interface, and dropping them into the appropriate location, you can upload your content efficiently. Let's break this process down step by step, explore its benefits, and provide practical tips to make drag-and-drop uploads more effective.

How Drag-and-Drop Uploads Work

Drag-and-drop functionality works by allowing users to interact with files and folders directly through their operating system or browser. Whether you're using the OneDrive web interface or the desktop application, you can upload content with a simple click, drag, and release action.

The Basics of Drag-and-Drop

1. **Selecting the Files or Folders**

    o   Navigate to the location on your computer where the files or folders are stored.

○ Click on a single file to select it. If you want to select multiple files, hold down the **Ctrl (Windows)** or **Command (Mac)** key and click on each file you want to upload. For selecting a series of consecutive files, hold down the **Shift key** and click the first and last file in the series.

2. **Dragging the Files**

○ Once your files are selected, click and hold the mouse button on any of the selected files.

○ While holding the mouse button, drag the files to the open OneDrive window or desktop folder location.

3. **Dropping the Files**

○ Move your cursor to the desired folder or area within OneDrive.

○ You'll usually see a visual cue, such as a highlighted border or a message like "Drop here to upload."

○ Release the mouse button to drop the files into the folder. The upload process will begin automatically.

Where to Use Drag-and-Drop

The drag-and-drop feature works seamlessly across various platforms. Let's explore where you can use this method:

1. OneDrive Web Interface

• Open your web browser and go to onedrive.live.com.

• Log in to your Microsoft account.

• Navigate to the folder where you want to upload your files.

• Open a File Explorer (Windows) or Finder (Mac) window on your computer.

• Drag the selected files from your computer into the OneDrive web browser window.

The upload progress bar will appear at the top of the screen, showing the number of files uploaded, the upload speed, and the remaining time. Once the process is complete, you'll see the files listed in the chosen folder.

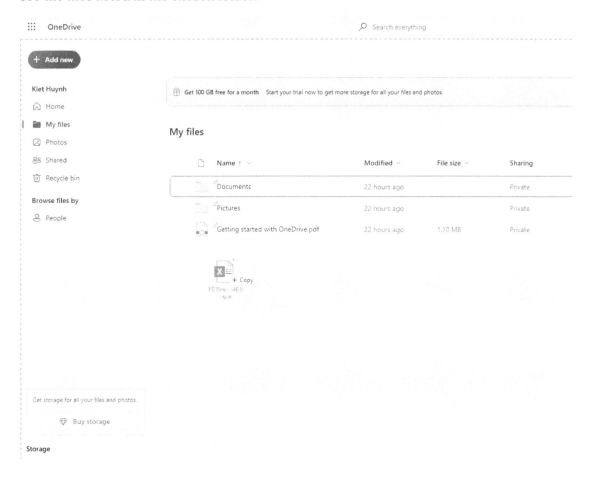

	Name ↑ ∨	Modified ∨	File size ∨	Sharing
	Documents	22 hours ago		Private
	Pictures	22 hours ago		Private
	FS THe - V6.3 - test.xlsx	Less than a minute ...	8.51 MB	Private
	Getting started with OneDrive.pdf	22 hours ago	1.10 MB	Private

Uploaded **FS THe - V6.3 - test.xlsx** to My files   ✕

2. OneDrive Desktop Application

If you're using the OneDrive desktop app (available for Windows and macOS), drag-and-drop uploads can be performed directly within the OneDrive folder on your computer.

- Locate the OneDrive folder in your File Explorer (Windows) or Finder (Mac).

- Open the OneDrive folder or any sub-folder where you want the files stored.

- Select the files from another location on your computer and drag them into the OneDrive folder.

The desktop app automatically syncs the files to the cloud. You'll notice a blue syncing icon next to the file name, which will turn into a green checkmark once the upload is complete.

3. OneDrive Mobile App

While drag-and-drop functionality is primarily used on computers, some mobile devices, especially tablets, also allow basic drag-and-drop actions within file management apps. For example, on iPadOS or Android tablets, you can:

- Open your Files app and the OneDrive app side by side in split view.

- Drag files from the Files app into OneDrive.

This is particularly useful for managing documents, images, or downloads on mobile devices.

Benefits of Using Drag-and-Drop Uploads

1. **Speed and Simplicity**
   Drag-and-drop is faster than navigating through menus to find an upload button. This method streamlines the process, especially when uploading multiple files at once.

2. **Intuitive Workflow**
   For users familiar with file management on their operating system, drag-and-drop feels natural and easy to use, requiring minimal instruction or setup.

3. **Multiple File Uploads**
   OneDrive supports bulk uploads using drag-and-drop. You can add entire folders or hundreds of files in one action, saving time compared to selecting files individually.

4. **Visual Feedback**
   The upload process provides clear visual indicators, such as progress bars, folder highlights, and success notifications, so users know exactly what's happening.

5. **Cross-Platform Support**
   Whether you're on Windows, Mac, or a web browser, the drag-and-drop functionality works consistently, ensuring a smooth experience across devices.

Practical Tips for Effective Drag-and-Drop Uploads

1. **Organize Before Uploading**
   Before dragging and dropping files into OneDrive, consider organizing them into

folders on your computer. This will help maintain a clean and structured file system in the cloud.

2. **Use Stable Internet Connections**

A stable internet connection ensures faster and error-free uploads. If your connection is interrupted, OneDrive may pause the upload and resume when the connection is restored.

3. **Monitor File Sizes**

While OneDrive allows large file uploads (up to 250 GB per file for premium accounts), dragging very large files may take longer. Be mindful of your internet bandwidth when handling big uploads.

4. **Check Sync Status**

For desktop uploads, ensure that the OneDrive app is running and syncing properly. Look for the sync icon in the taskbar (Windows) or menu bar (Mac).

5. **Avoid Overwriting Files**

If a file with the same name already exists in the target folder, OneDrive may prompt you to choose whether to overwrite the file, create a duplicate, or cancel the upload. Pay attention to these prompts to avoid mistakes.

6. **Test Large Batches**

If you're uploading hundreds of files, consider testing with a small batch first to ensure the upload process is smooth and your connection is stable.

Common Issues and Troubleshooting for Drag-and-Drop Uploads

1. Drag-and-Drop Not Working

- Ensure that you're using a supported web browser (e.g., Chrome, Edge, Safari). Outdated browsers may not support drag-and-drop functionality.

- Clear your browser cache and restart the browser.

2. Upload Stuck or Failed

- Check your internet connection. Upload interruptions often occur due to weak or unstable connections.

- Verify file size limits. Files exceeding the OneDrive upload limit will fail to upload.

3. Files Not Syncing to the Cloud

- If you're using the desktop app, check the OneDrive sync status. Pause and resume syncing if necessary.

- Restart the OneDrive app to refresh the connection.

4. Browser Freezing

- Dragging and dropping large batches of files may cause your browser to slow down or freeze temporarily. Consider splitting files into smaller groups.

Conclusion

The drag-and-drop upload method in OneDrive offers a seamless and efficient way to manage your files. Whether you're adding individual documents, folders, or large batches of files, this method provides a user-friendly and intuitive experience. By understanding its basics, benefits, and practical tips, you can streamline your workflow, organize your cloud storage effectively, and maximize your productivity with OneDrive.

In the next section, we'll explore how to upload files using the **Upload Button**, another handy method for managing your OneDrive content.

2.1.2 Using the Upload Button

Uploading files and folders to OneDrive using the **Upload Button** is one of the most straightforward and user-friendly ways to manage your digital content. The Upload Button provides a clear and consistent method for adding files to your cloud storage, regardless of the device or platform you are using. This section will guide you step-by-step on how to use this feature, explore the options it provides, and address common questions or issues you may encounter.

What Is the Upload Button and Where to Find It?

The **Upload Button** is a key feature in OneDrive, allowing users to transfer files or entire folders from their local devices (computers, tablets, or smartphones) directly into the cloud. It is available in the following versions of OneDrive:

1. **Web Version (OneDrive Online):** Located at the top menu bar, usually labeled as "Upload" with an arrow pointing upwards.

2. **Desktop Application:** Files can also be added via the Upload menu when using the OneDrive sync client.

3. **Mobile Apps (iOS/Android):** Found under the "+" or "Add" icon in the bottom menu.

The **Upload Button** provides options for uploading:

- **Individual Files** – Single documents, images, or other types of files.

- **Multiple Files** – Select multiple files at once for bulk upload.

- **Folders** – Upload entire directories, including their subfolders and contents.

Let's break down how you can use the Upload Button across different platforms.

Step-by-Step Guide: Uploading Files and Folders on the Web Version

+ Add new

Folder

Files upload

Folder upload

Word document

Excel workbook

PowerPoint presentation

OneNote notebook

Excel survey

Text Document

1. **Access OneDrive Online:**

   o   Open a web browser and visit onedrive.live.com.

   o   Log in with your Microsoft account credentials (email and password).

2. **Locate the Upload Button:**

   o   Once logged in, the main interface displays the toolbar at the top of the screen.

   o   The **Upload** button will appear with an upward-pointing arrow icon.

3. **Upload Individual Files:**

   o   Click on the **Upload** button. A dropdown menu will appear with two options:

   ▪   **Files**

   ▪   **Folder**

   o   Choose **Files**. This action will open the file explorer (on Windows) or Finder (on macOS).

   o   Navigate to the location of the file you want to upload. Select the file and click **Open**.

   o   OneDrive will upload the selected file, and a small status bar will appear at the top of the screen indicating the upload progress.

4. **Upload an Entire Folder:**

   o   Click the **Upload** button again and select **Folder** from the dropdown menu.

   o   Navigate to the folder you want to upload in the file explorer or Finder.

   o   Select the folder and confirm by clicking **Upload** or **Open**.

   o   The upload process will begin, and OneDrive will transfer all the folder's contents, including subfolders.

5. **Monitor Upload Progress:**

   o   While the file(s) or folder(s) are uploading, a progress bar will appear in the upper-right corner.

- o   You can continue browsing your OneDrive while the upload completes.

6. **Verify Upload Completion:**

- o   Once the upload is finished, you'll receive a notification in the upper corner.

- o   The uploaded file(s) or folder(s) will appear in your current directory. If needed, you can refresh the page to ensure all content is visible.

Using the Upload Button on the Desktop Application

If you are using the OneDrive desktop application on Windows or macOS, uploading files is just as simple.

1. **Access the OneDrive Folder:**

- o   Once the OneDrive sync client is installed, it integrates with your file explorer (Windows) or Finder (macOS).

- o   Open the OneDrive folder in the file explorer or Finder.

2. **Upload via Right-Click Option:**

- o   Right-click anywhere inside the OneDrive folder.

- o   Select **Upload** or **Add Files** (based on system options).

3. **Drag-and-Drop Alternative:**

- o   While not directly involving the "Upload Button," you can drag files from any local directory into the OneDrive folder to begin the sync process.

The desktop app automatically uploads any files or folders placed in the OneDrive directory to the cloud.

Uploading Files and Folders on Mobile Devices

Using the **OneDrive Mobile App** (available for both Android and iOS) offers a convenient way to upload files directly from your smartphone or tablet.

1. **Open the OneDrive Mobile App:**

- o   Log in to your account if you haven't already.

2. **Locate the Upload Feature:**

   o Tap the **"+"** icon at the bottom of the screen.

   o Choose **Upload** from the available options.

3. **Upload Files:**

   o Navigate through your phone's storage to find the file(s) you want to upload.

   o Select the file(s) and tap **Upload**.

4. **Upload Photos Automatically:**

   o For convenience, OneDrive can automatically upload photos taken with your phone. To enable this feature:

     ▪ Go to **Settings** in the app.

     ▪ Turn on **Camera Upload**.

5. **Upload Folders:**

   o While some mobile versions restrict full-folder uploads, you can create a new folder in the app and add files to it individually.

Tips for Efficient File Uploads

- **Use a Stable Internet Connection:** A strong and steady internet connection ensures that your uploads are quick and uninterrupted.

- **Upload in Batches:** Instead of uploading hundreds of files at once, group files into smaller batches to reduce the risk of errors.

- **Avoid Large File Sizes on Limited Plans:** If your OneDrive plan has limited storage, monitor file sizes before uploading. Large video files, for example, might consume significant space.

- **Enable Notifications:** Turn on notifications in OneDrive to get updates about upload progress or failures.

Common Upload Issues and Solutions

1. **Upload Button Not Working:**

   o **Solution:** Refresh the page or log out and back into your account. Check your internet connection.

2. **File Size Limit Exceeded:**

   o Free accounts have a file upload limit of 100GB. If a file exceeds this, split it into smaller parts or upgrade your OneDrive plan.

3. **Corrupted Files:**

   o Ensure the file is not corrupted before uploading. Test opening it locally first.

4. **Slow Upload Speeds:**

   o Close other programs consuming bandwidth or upload during off-peak hours.

Conclusion: Mastering the Upload Button

The **Upload Button** in OneDrive offers an intuitive and seamless method to transfer files and folders to the cloud. Whether you are using the web version, desktop client, or mobile app, the process is simple and efficient. By understanding where to locate the Upload Button and how to use it effectively, you can ensure that your digital content is safely stored, accessible, and organized in OneDrive.

Mastering this fundamental feature will make it easier to manage your files, collaborate with others, and keep your data secure across devices.

2.2 Organizing Your Files

2.2.1 Creating Folders

Creating folders in OneDrive is a fundamental step in organizing your files effectively. Folders act as containers that help group related files together, ensuring a clean, structured layout for easy navigation and quick access. Whether you're using OneDrive for personal files, professional documents, or collaborative projects, mastering folder creation will save you time and enhance productivity.

This section will guide you through the different methods for creating folders across OneDrive platforms (web, desktop, and mobile) and provide tips for naming conventions, folder hierarchies, and overall organization best practices.

Creating Folders on the OneDrive Web App

The web version of OneDrive is a convenient way to create and organize folders, particularly if you're accessing your files through a browser. Follow these steps to create a folder:

1. **Navigate to OneDrive**

   o   Open your preferred web browser.

   o   Go to onedrive.live.com and log in with your Microsoft account credentials.

   o   Once you are on the OneDrive homepage, you'll see a clean, organized interface with your existing folders and files.

2. **Locate the "New" Button**

   o   At the top of the interface, you will see the toolbar.

   o   Click on the **"New"** button, which appears on the left side of the toolbar. This button opens a drop-down menu with several options.

3. **Select "Folder"**

   o   From the drop-down list, select **"Folder."**

○   A small dialog box will appear, prompting you to name your new folder.

4. Enter a Folder Name

○   Enter a clear and descriptive name for your folder. For example, instead of generic names like "Folder1," use names like "Work Documents," "Vacation Photos 2024," or "Invoices - Q1 2024."

○   Press **Enter** or click **"Create"** to finalize the process.

5. Locate Your Folder

○   Your new folder will appear in the current directory. You can now click into the folder to add files, create subfolders, or share the folder with others.

Creating Folders in the OneDrive Desktop Application

The OneDrive desktop application offers seamless integration with Windows File Explorer or Mac Finder. This option is particularly useful if you prefer organizing files directly from your computer's native file system.

On Windows

1. Ensure OneDrive Sync is Active

○   Open the OneDrive app on your computer and sign in if prompted.

○   The synced OneDrive folder will appear in File Explorer under the "OneDrive" section in the left pane.

2. Navigate to Your Desired Location

- o Open your OneDrive folder in File Explorer.

- o Browse to the location where you want to create a new folder (e.g., root directory, inside an existing folder).

3. **Create a New Folder**

- o Right-click in the desired location.

- o Select **"New"** from the context menu.

- o Click on **"Folder."**

4. **Name Your Folder**

- o A folder icon will appear with a blank name field.

- o Type a descriptive name for your folder and press **Enter** to save it.

5. **Verify Syncing**

- o Once the folder is created, a small green checkmark icon will appear on the folder. This indicates that the folder has been synced with your OneDrive cloud storage.

On Mac

1. **Open Finder**

- o Locate the OneDrive folder in Finder (under "Locations" or "Favorites").

2. **Create the Folder**

- o Right-click in the desired location.

- o Select **"New Folder."**

3. **Name and Verify**

- o Enter a folder name and confirm. A synced OneDrive folder will also show a status icon to indicate successful sync.

Creating Folders in the OneDrive Mobile App

OneDrive's mobile app (available for iOS and Android) is perfect for creating and managing folders on the go. Here's how:

1. **Open the OneDrive App**

   o   Launch the OneDrive app on your smartphone or tablet.

   o   Sign in if prompted.

2. **Navigate to the Desired Location**

   o   Browse through your files and folders to the location where you want to create a new folder.

3. **Tap on the "+" Button**

   o   At the top or bottom of the screen, you'll see a **"+"** (Create) button. Tap on it to open a menu.

4. **Select "Create Folder"**

   o   From the menu, choose the **"Create Folder"** option.

5. **Name Your Folder**

   o   Enter a name for your new folder and tap **"Create"** or **"Done."**

6. **View Your Folder**

   o   The new folder will immediately appear in the location you selected. You can now upload files directly into it or create subfolders.

Best Practices for Folder Organization

Creating folders is just the first step toward an organized file system. Here are some best practices for keeping your OneDrive folders tidy and easy to navigate:

1. Use Clear and Consistent Naming Conventions

- **Be Descriptive:** Avoid vague folder names like "Stuff" or "New Folder." Use descriptive names that explain the folder's contents (e.g., "Project Alpha Reports," "Family Photos 2023").

- **Include Dates:** For time-sensitive files, add dates or timeframes to folder names (e.g., "Invoices Q1 2024," "Meeting Notes - May 2024").

- **Stick to a Format:** Establish a naming convention such as:

  o [Category] - [Description] - [Date] (e.g., "Work - Marketing Plan - 2024").

  o [Project Name] > [Phase] > [Details].

2. Create Folder Hierarchies

Instead of cramming everything into a single folder, build a logical hierarchy:

- **Root Folder:** Start with broad categories (e.g., "Work," "Personal," "Finance").

- **Subfolders:** Break down broad categories into smaller sections (e.g., "Work > Reports > Monthly Reports").

- **Nested Folders:** Add deeper levels only when necessary. Avoid over-nesting as it may complicate navigation.

3. Use Tags and Metadata for Additional Organization

- Tags or keywords make it easier to search for files. Add tags where possible, especially if your folders contain numerous documents.

4. Review and Declutter Regularly

Periodically review your folders to remove outdated files, reorganize messy directories, and archive older folders that you no longer need immediate access to.

Common Mistakes to Avoid When Creating Folders

- **Overcomplicating the Structure:** Creating too many levels of subfolders can make it difficult to locate files.

- **Not Renaming Default Folders:** Always rename "New Folder" to something specific to avoid confusion.

- **Inconsistent Naming:** Using different naming styles can make it hard to search and navigate files later.

- **Skipping Organization Steps:** Uploading files without placing them in appropriate folders will lead to clutter over time.

By following these steps and best practices, you can ensure your OneDrive is clean, organized, and efficient. Folders are the backbone of a well-structured file management system, allowing you to focus on work without wasting time searching for files. Now that you've mastered folder creation, the next section will cover how to rename, move, and manage your files for even better organization.

2.2.2 Renaming and Moving Items

Organizing files is a crucial step to maintaining a clean and efficient workspace in OneDrive. Whether you are managing personal files, work documents, or shared content, renaming and moving items are essential skills that will help you stay organized and find what you need when you need it. In this section, we'll explore the specific techniques and best practices for renaming and relocating files and folders in OneDrive, across all available platforms: desktop, web, and mobile.

Why Rename and Move Items?

Before diving into the "how-to," it's important to understand the *why*:

1. **Improved Organization**: Clear and specific file names make it easy to identify content at a glance. Moving items into appropriate folders keeps your storage organized.

2. **Ease of Search**: Descriptive names improve searchability in OneDrive, saving time when retrieving files.

3. **Better Collaboration**: When sharing files or folders, consistent and clear names help others locate and understand content quickly.

4. **Avoid Duplication**: Proper naming reduces the risk of creating duplicates and confusing versions of files.

5. **Professionalism**: Clean naming conventions and organized structures are especially important in a professional setting.

Renaming Files and Folders

Renaming a file or folder in OneDrive is a straightforward process, but the method depends on the platform you are using. Below, we'll discuss how to rename content using the web version, the desktop app, and the mobile app.

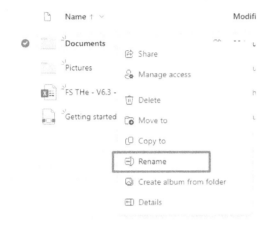

Renaming in OneDrive on the Web

1. **Log In to OneDrive**: Open your preferred browser, navigate to <u>onedrive.live.com</u>, and log in with your Microsoft account.

2. **Locate the File or Folder**: Browse to the file or folder you want to rename.

3. **Right-Click and Select "Rename"**: Right-click the item, and from the dropdown menu, select **Rename**.

4. **Enter the New Name**: A text box will appear around the current name. Type the new name and press **Enter** or click anywhere outside the text box to save.

Alternatively:

- **Select the File**: Click the checkbox next to the file or folder.

- **Choose the "Rename" Option**: In the top toolbar, select the **Rename** button.

- Follow the same process to enter and confirm the new name.

Tips for Web Renaming:

- Use clear, descriptive names (e.g., "Annual_Report_2023" instead of "report_final").

- Avoid special characters like ":", "*", "?", as these are unsupported in file names.

Renaming in the OneDrive Desktop App

The OneDrive desktop app seamlessly integrates with your computer's file explorer, allowing you to manage files and folders just like any other local content.

1. **Open File Explorer (Windows) or Finder (Mac)**: Navigate to your OneDrive folder. It will appear under "OneDrive" in the left-hand navigation pane.

2. **Locate the File or Folder**: Find the item you want to rename.

3. **Right-Click and Select "Rename"**:

   o On Windows: Right-click the file or folder, then choose **Rename**.

   o On Mac: Right-click (or two-finger click) the item, then select **Rename**.

4. **Enter the New Name**: Highlight the current name, type the new name, and press **Enter**.

Keyboard Shortcut:

- Windows users can select the file and press **F2** to rename instantly.

- Mac users can select the file and press the **Return (Enter)** key.

Renaming in the OneDrive Mobile App

OneDrive's mobile app allows you to manage your files on the go. Renaming files is just as simple on a smartphone or tablet.

1. **Open the OneDrive App**: Launch the app on your iOS or Android device.

2. **Locate the File or Folder**: Navigate to the file or folder you wish to rename.

3. **Tap the Three-Dot Menu**: Tap the **three-dot icon** (⋯) next to the file name to open additional options.

4. **Choose "Rename"**: Select the **Rename** option from the menu.

5. **Enter the New Name**: Type the desired name, and tap **Save** or **OK** to confirm.

Note: Ensure that you have a stable internet connection to avoid delays in syncing changes back to OneDrive.

Best Practices for Renaming Files

To make the most of the renaming feature, consider the following best practices:

1. **Be Descriptive and Specific**:
   - Example: Instead of "Document1.pdf," use "Client_Proposal_March2024.pdf."
   - This makes it easier to identify the file's purpose without opening it.

2. **Use Consistent Naming Conventions**:
   - For personal files: Use dates or events (e.g., "Vacation_Photos_Italy2024").
   - For professional files: Follow organizational guidelines like "ProjectName_Type_Date" (e.g., "XYZCorp_Report_April2024").

3. **Include Dates When Relevant**: Add dates in the format YYYY-MM-DD to maintain chronological order.
   - Example: "2024-03-15_MeetingNotes.docx."

4. **Avoid Special Characters**: Stick to alphanumeric characters, hyphens (-), and underscores (_).

5. **Review and Rename Periodically**: Regularly audit your files to ensure names remain relevant and easy to navigate.

Moving Files and Folders

Moving files and folders in OneDrive allows you to restructure your storage, keeping related items together for easy access. You can move content within OneDrive or between folders and devices.

Moving Files and Folders in OneDrive on the Web

1. **Select the File or Folder**: Hover over the item, click the checkbox next to it, or right-click to highlight it.

2. **Choose "Move To"**: In the toolbar above, click **Move to**.

3. **Select the Destination**: A panel will open, displaying your folder structure. Navigate to the target folder.

4. **Confirm the Move**: Click **Move here** to complete the process.

Moving Files Using Drag-and-Drop

OneDrive's web interface also allows drag-and-drop functionality for a more visual experience:

1. **Navigate to the File**: Locate the file or folder you want to move.

2. **Click and Hold the Item**: Drag the file over to the target folder.

3. **Release to Drop**: Once the folder is highlighted, release the mouse button to complete the move.

Moving Files in the Desktop App

Moving files and folders in the desktop app mirrors the experience of working with local files:

1. **Open File Explorer or Finder**: Navigate to your OneDrive folder.

2. **Cut and Paste**:

    o On Windows: Right-click the file, select **Cut**, navigate to the destination folder, and select **Paste**.

    o On Mac: Right-click the file, choose **Move To**, and select the destination.

3. **Drag-and-Drop**: You can also drag files from one folder to another, as you would with any local storage.

Moving Files in the Mobile App

1. **Locate the File or Folder**: Navigate to the file you want to move.

2. **Tap the Three-Dot Menu**: Select **Move** from the options.

3. **Choose a Destination**: Browse to the target folder.

4. **Confirm the Move**: Tap **Move Here** to complete the action.

Best Practices for Moving Items

1. **Create a Folder Structure Before Moving**: Organize your folder system first to avoid confusion.

2. **Use Clear Folder Names**: Ensure that folder names describe their content (e.g., "Invoices_2024" or "Personal_Photos_Trips").

3. **Batch Move Files**: Select multiple files at once for efficient organization.

4. **Check for Duplicates**: Before moving, ensure there are no duplicate versions of files in the destination folder.

Conclusion

Renaming and moving files and folders are simple but powerful actions that keep your OneDrive storage clean, accessible, and professional. By following consistent naming conventions and organizing content into logical folders, you can maximize efficiency and minimize clutter. Whether you are using OneDrive for personal or professional purposes, these tools empower you to manage files effectively across all devices.

2.2.3 Using Tags and Metadata

In today's digital landscape, organizing files effectively is crucial for productivity and efficiency. While creating folders and renaming files is a great start, using tags and metadata can take your OneDrive file organization to the next level. Tags and metadata allow you to classify and retrieve your files quickly without relying solely on folder structures. This approach is particularly useful when dealing with a large volume of documents or files that belong to multiple categories or projects.

This section will explore what tags and metadata are, how to use them in OneDrive, and practical strategies for leveraging these features to streamline file management.

Understanding Tags and Metadata

Before diving into the details of using tags and metadata in OneDrive, let's define these terms:

- **Tags:** Tags are keywords or labels you can attach to files or folders. They provide a way to categorize or identify files quickly based on their content, project, or purpose. Unlike folders, tags allow you to assign multiple keywords to a single file. For example, a report about your marketing strategy could be tagged with keywords like *"Q4 Marketing," "Strategy Report,"* and *"2024."*

- **Metadata:** Metadata is data about your data. In OneDrive, metadata includes attributes like file name, file size, date created, date modified, author, and even custom properties such as tags. It helps you understand and organize your files beyond the name and folder structure.

The combination of tags and metadata empowers you to find what you need quickly, even if you don't remember the exact file name or its location. For instance, searching for a file tagged "invoice" will retrieve all documents labeled with this tag, regardless of the folder in which they are stored.

Why Use Tags and Metadata in OneDrive?

There are several benefits to using tags and metadata:

1. **Improved Search Efficiency**: Tags make it easier to locate files using search filters or keywords. Rather than browsing through multiple folders, you can type a tag in the search bar to quickly retrieve relevant results.

2. **Flexible Organization**: Tags provide flexibility that folder structures do not. A single file can belong to multiple categories, and you don't need to duplicate it in multiple folders.

3. **Enhanced Collaboration**: Tags make shared file libraries easier to navigate. Your team members can use consistent tags to label files, making it simple for everyone to find important documents.

4. **Saves Time**: With metadata, you can retrieve documents based on criteria like creation date, file type, or author. This saves time when searching for files with specific attributes.

5. **Scalability**: As the number of files in your OneDrive grows, managing them with folders alone becomes overwhelming. Tags and metadata allow for scalable and consistent organization.

How to Add and Use Tags in OneDrive

OneDrive supports tags in conjunction with Microsoft 365 and SharePoint integration. While basic tags can be manually added through properties, advanced tagging and metadata functionality are enhanced when used in business or enterprise OneDrive accounts.

Step 1: Adding Tags to Files

1. **Through File Properties**:

   o Navigate to the file you want to tag.

   o Right-click on the file and select **Details**.

   o Under the **Properties** section, look for a field like **Tags** or **Keywords** (depending on your version).

   o Add one or more relevant tags (separated by semicolons). For example: *"Invoice; Q4; 2024."*

   o Save your changes.

2. **Using Microsoft 365 Apps**:

    o   If you're editing a Word, Excel, or PowerPoint document stored in OneDrive, you can add tags directly from the document's **Properties** panel.

    o   Go to **File > Info**, and look for the **Tags** or **Keywords** field.

    o   Enter your desired tags and save the document.

3. **During Upload**:

○   When uploading a file to OneDrive, you can immediately add tags through the **Details** panel. After the file uploads, select it, open **Details**, and add relevant tags.

Step 2: Searching for Tagged Files

Once you've added tags to your files, finding them becomes effortless:

1. Open your OneDrive folder on the web or desktop app.

2. Use the **Search bar** at the top of the screen.

3. Type the relevant tag or keyword. For instance, searching *"Invoice"* will show all files tagged with "Invoice."

4. Filter results further by selecting additional search options such as file type, date modified, or author.

If your files are well-tagged, the search function becomes incredibly powerful, saving you from browsing through endless folders.

Step 3: Managing Tags for Consistency

To ensure consistency, especially in shared libraries or collaborative projects, consider the following tips:

1. **Create a Tagging Convention**:
    Develop a standard way to name and apply tags. For example:

    ○   Use singular nouns (e.g., *Report* instead of *Reports*).

    ○   Use year or quarter identifiers (e.g., *Q4_2024*).

    ○   Avoid using too many similar tags (e.g., *"Report," "Reports," "Docs"*).

2. **Share a Tag List**:
    In team settings, share a list of commonly used tags and encourage team members to follow it. This reduces duplication and confusion.

3. **Review and Clean Up Tags Regularly**:
   Periodically check your files for outdated or inconsistent tags. Remove unnecessary tags or merge duplicates where possible.

Using Metadata for Advanced File Organization

In addition to tags, metadata fields in OneDrive provide valuable information about your files. Here's how you can leverage metadata:

1. Viewing File Metadata

To view a file's metadata:

- Select the file and click on **Details** (on the right sidebar).

- You'll see attributes such as file name, file size, date created, date modified, and author.

For shared files, metadata also includes who last edited the file and when.

2. Custom Metadata Fields

If you're using OneDrive for Business, you can create custom metadata fields through SharePoint integration. Custom fields allow you to organize files based on attributes unique to your workflow.

For example:

- **Project Name**: Add a field to identify projects.

- **Client Name**: Categorize files by client.

- **Document Status**: Add fields like *Draft, In Review, Approved*.

To set up custom metadata:

1. Open your document library (via OneDrive or SharePoint).

2. Click **Library Settings** > **Create Column**.

3. Choose a column type (text, dropdown, etc.).

4. Enter a name for your field (e.g., *Project Name*).

3. Sorting and Filtering with Metadata

Once metadata fields are set up, you can sort and filter your files:

- Click on the column headers (e.g., *Project Name*) to sort files alphabetically.

- Use the **Filter** option to view files that meet specific criteria, such as *Status = Approved.*

Practical Use Cases for Tags and Metadata

Here are some real-world scenarios where tags and metadata shine:

- **Organizing Project Files**: Tag project-related documents with *Project Name, Status,* and *Deadline.*

- **Managing Invoices**: Use tags like *Invoice, Client Name,* and *Year.*

- **Tracking Meeting Notes**: Label meeting minutes with *Team Name* and *Date.*

- **Handling Shared Resources**: Assign tags like *Shared Files* or *Internal Only* for clarity.

Conclusion

Using tags and metadata in OneDrive can transform the way you manage and retrieve your files. While folders remain the backbone of file organization, tags add flexibility and power to your system. By implementing a consistent tagging strategy and leveraging metadata fields, you'll save time, enhance collaboration, and maintain a scalable organization system as your file library grows. Whether you're managing personal documents or collaborating on team projects, mastering tags and metadata will ensure your OneDrive stays organized and efficient.

2.3 Searching and Sorting

2.3.1 Search Bar Basics

$\mathcal{P}$ Search everything

OneDrive provides a robust search function that allows you to locate files and folders quickly, even within large collections of data. Whether you're accessing files via the OneDrive desktop app, web interface, or mobile application, the search bar offers an intuitive and efficient way to find what you need. This section will explain how to use the search bar effectively, explore the different features it offers, and provide tips to maximize your search efficiency.

Understanding the Search Bar in OneDrive

The search bar is a key feature located prominently within the OneDrive interface. Depending on the platform you're using, it may appear slightly different but serves the same purpose: to locate files, folders, or specific content based on keywords.

- **Web Version**: On the web version of OneDrive (via your browser), the search bar is usually found at the top center of the screen, just above your file list. Typing into this bar will allow you to search within your files and folders seamlessly.

- **Desktop App**: In the Windows File Explorer or macOS Finder, the search function integrates with the operating system's native tools, allowing you to search directly from your file manager.

- **Mobile App**: On the OneDrive mobile application, the search bar is often represented by a magnifying glass icon. It is accessible by tapping the icon at the top of the screen.

Regardless of the platform, the search function provides instant suggestions as you type and helps you narrow down your results.

How to Use the Search Bar

Using the search bar in OneDrive is straightforward, but understanding its features will help you locate files faster and more accurately. Here's a step-by-step guide:

1. **Locate the Search Bar**: As mentioned, find the search bar at the top of the screen in the web and mobile apps or use the built-in search function in your desktop file manager.

2. **Type Keywords**: Start typing the name of the file, folder, or content you're looking for. The search bar will offer **real-time suggestions** based on what you type.

3. **Select a Result**: As you type, the search will display relevant results instantly. You can click or tap on a suggested file to open it directly.

4. **Refine Your Search**: If the search results don't show what you're looking for immediately, press *Enter* or tap *Search* to view the full list of matches. Use filters to narrow down the results further (covered later in this chapter).

For example:

- If you type "Budget," OneDrive will display any files or folders with the word "Budget" in the title, content, or metadata.

- You can search for parts of a file name, such as "2024," and OneDrive will return all items with "2024" anywhere in their names.

What Can You Search For?

The OneDrive search bar is not limited to file names; it can search for various types of data. Here's a breakdown of what you can search for using this feature:

1. **File Names**: The most common use of the search bar is to locate files by name. For instance, typing "Project Proposal" will bring up all files and folders containing that exact phrase.

2. **Folder Names**: If you're looking for an entire folder, you can type its name, and OneDrive will display it along with any related subfolders.

3. **File Types**: Searching for a specific file extension like ".docx" or ".pdf" will filter your results to only show those file types.

4. **Content Inside Files**: OneDrive can search for text **within documents** such as Word, Excel, and PowerPoint files. For instance, if you type "Sales Report,"

OneDrive will locate documents containing those words even if the file title doesn't include them.

5. **Metadata**: Metadata refers to details about your files, such as tags, dates, or owners. If you've added tags to your files, you can search using those keywords.

6. **Shared Items**: The search bar will also display files or folders that others have shared with you.

Real-Time Suggestions and Auto-Complete

As you type into the search bar, OneDrive provides real-time suggestions that aim to match what you're looking for. These suggestions save time by offering immediate access to relevant results.

For example:

- Typing "Meeting" might show results such as *"Meeting Notes.docx"*, *"Weekly Meeting Agenda.pdf"*, or *"2024 Sales Meeting"*.

- Auto-complete will fill in common keywords based on your past searches or file history.

To use these suggestions effectively:

- Start typing slowly and observe the drop-down list of results.

- Select the file or folder that matches what you need.

- If no matches appear, press *Enter* to perform a broader search.

Tips for Effective Searching

To make the most of the search bar, consider the following tips and strategies:

1. **Use Specific Keywords**: Be as specific as possible when typing keywords. For instance, instead of "Report," try "Q1 Sales Report 2024."

2. **Search for File Extensions**: If you're looking for a specific type of file, such as a spreadsheet, include the file extension (e.g., ".xlsx" or ".pdf").

3. **Capitalize on Partial Matches**: You don't need to type the full file name. Searching for "Proj" will display results like "Project Proposal" or "Project Plan."

4. **Combine Keywords**: Use multiple keywords to narrow down your results. For example, "Budget 2024" will refine your search to items containing both words.

5. **Leverage Tags**: If you've tagged your files, include the tags as search terms. Tags help you organize and find files faster.

6. **Search by Owner**: If you share a lot of files, searching by the name of the person who created or shared the file can help.

Common Scenarios for Using the Search Bar

Here are a few practical examples of how the search bar can streamline your work:

1. **Locating Old Files**: Suppose you're looking for last year's performance review but can't remember the exact name. Simply search for "Review 2023" to find the relevant document.

2. **Finding Shared Content**: If a colleague shared a presentation with you but you can't remember where it's stored, search for keywords like "Presentation" or their name.

3. **Searching by Date**: To find files modified recently, use filters alongside the search bar to show files from a specific time period.

Limitations of the Search Bar

While OneDrive's search functionality is powerful, it does have some limitations:

- **File Content Search**: Searching for content within files works well for Microsoft Office formats like Word, Excel, and PowerPoint but may be limited for non-Microsoft file types.

- **Shared File Confusion**: If many users share files with similar names, distinguishing between them can be challenging. Adding tags or renaming files can help.

- **Case Sensitivity**: While OneDrive search is not case-sensitive, using proper capitalization can improve readability when reviewing search results.

Final Thoughts on Mastering the Search Bar

The search bar is an essential tool in OneDrive that allows you to manage and locate files quickly, saving valuable time. By understanding its features and following best practices, you can transform how you organize and access your data. Whether you're searching for a specific file, folder, or even text within a document, OneDrive's search bar ensures your files are always just a few keystrokes away.

In the next section, we will explore **Advanced Filtering Options**, which provide additional ways to narrow down your search results for even greater precision.

2.3.2 Advanced Filtering Options

Organizing files in OneDrive can become overwhelming as your storage grows. Searching is a great tool to locate files quickly, but sometimes a simple keyword search isn't enough. That's where advanced filtering options come in. OneDrive offers a robust set of filtering tools that allow you to narrow down search results and locate files based on specific attributes like file type, modified date, owner, and shared status.

In this section, you will learn:

- How to use advanced filters to locate files efficiently.

- The types of filtering options available.

- Real-life scenarios where advanced filtering can save time and improve productivity.

1. Why Use Advanced Filters?

As your OneDrive usage increases, you may end up with hundreds or even thousands of files, including documents, images, videos, and PDFs. Navigating through these files manually is neither efficient nor practical. Advanced filtering helps by:

- **Saving Time**: Quickly locate the exact file you need without scrolling through multiple folders.

- **Improving Accuracy**: Filters ensure you find the right file by specifying its type, last modified date, or owner.

- **Simplifying Collaboration**: Find files that were shared with you or that you have shared with others.

Whether you're a student searching for a final report, a business professional locating an invoice, or a photographer organizing thousands of images, advanced filters in OneDrive simplify file management.

2. Accessing Advanced Filters

To use advanced filtering options in OneDrive:

1. Open **OneDrive** via the web browser or mobile app.

2. Click on the **Search Bar** at the top of the screen.

3. A dropdown menu will appear with initial suggestions and recent files. Below the suggestions, look for the **Filter Options** icon or "Advanced Filters" button.

4. Click on it to expand the filtering menu.

The filtering panel typically includes the following options:

- **File Type**

- **Modified Date**

- **File Size**

- **Shared With**

- **Owner**

These filters can be used individually or in combination to narrow your search results effectively.

3. Types of Advanced Filtering Options

Let's dive into each of the advanced filters available and how you can use them effectively.

3.1 Filter by File Type

Filtering by file type allows you to limit search results to a specific category, such as documents, images, videos, or PDFs.

- **Steps to Filter by File Type**:
    - ○ Open the advanced filter menu.
    - ○ Locate the **File Type** dropdown menu.
    - ○ Select the file type you are searching for (e.g., Word Documents, Excel Files, Images, PDFs, Videos).
    - ○ The search results will immediately update to show only files of the selected type.

- **Common File Types Supported**:
    - ○ **Documents**: Word, Excel, PowerPoint, Google Docs.
    - ○ **Images**: JPEG, PNG, GIF, TIFF.
    - ○ **Videos**: MP4, AVI, MOV.
    - ○ **PDFs**: Portable Document Format files.
    - ○ **Audio Files**: MP3, WAV.

- **Use Case Example**:

    Imagine you're preparing a presentation and need to gather all your slides. By filtering by **PowerPoint Files (.pptx)**, you can instantly view all relevant presentations without the distraction of other file types.

3.2 Filter by Modified Date

The "Modified Date" filter helps you find files based on when they were last edited or uploaded.

- **Steps to Filter by Modified Date**:

o In the advanced filter menu, find the **Modified Date** option.

o Select one of the preset date ranges:

▪ **Today**

▪ **Yesterday**

▪ **This Week**

▪ **This Month**

▪ **Custom Range** (to specify exact start and end dates).

o The search results will automatically adjust to include only files modified within the selected timeframe.

- **Use Case Example**:

Suppose you were working on a report last week and can't remember the file name. By selecting **"This Week"** under Modified Date, you can filter out older files and narrow down your options quickly.

3.3 Filter by File Size

For users with limited storage space, filtering by file size is particularly useful. This filter allows you to locate large files that might be taking up valuable space in your OneDrive.

- **Steps to Filter by File Size**:

o Open the advanced filter menu and locate the **File Size** option.

o Use the predefined ranges to filter files:

▪ **Small (0–10 MB)**

▪ **Medium (10–100 MB)**

▪ **Large (100 MB–1 GB)**

▪ **Extra Large (>1 GB)**

o You can also input a custom file size range if needed.

- **Use Case Example**:

If you're running out of space on your free OneDrive account, filtering for **Large** or **Extra Large** files can help you quickly identify files that you no longer need, allowing you to free up space efficiently.

3.4 Filter by Shared With

The "Shared With" filter is particularly useful when you're collaborating on files with multiple people. It allows you to filter files based on who has access to them.

- **Steps to Filter by Shared With**:

    o In the filter menu, find the **Shared With** field.

    o Enter the name or email address of the person you've shared files with or who shared files with you.

    o The results will show only files that involve the specified person.

- **Use Case Example**:

    If a colleague sent you multiple files last month, but you need to locate a specific one, simply filter by their name to view all files shared between you two.

3.5 Filter by Owner

Filtering by owner is particularly helpful in collaborative workspaces where files are owned by different team members.

- **Steps to Filter by Owner**:

    o In the advanced filter menu, locate the **Owner** option.

    o Enter the name or email address of the file's owner.

    o The results will update to show files owned by that person.

- **Use Case Example**:

    If you're searching for a report that was uploaded by your manager, simply filter files by their name or email to quickly locate the file.

4. Combining Multiple Filters

OneDrive allows you to combine multiple filters for a more precise search. For example, you can filter files that:

- Are PDFs **(File Type: PDF)**
- Were modified **last month (Modified Date)**
- Were shared by a specific team member **(Shared With)**

Steps to Combine Filters:

1. Open the advanced filter menu.
2. Select the filters you want to apply (e.g., File Type + Modified Date).
3. Refine the filters further by adding File Size or Shared With options.
4. View the updated search results.

Example Scenario:

Imagine you're searching for a large PDF report shared by a team member last month. By selecting **"File Type: PDF"**, **"Modified Date: Last Month"**, and adding their name under **"Shared With"**, you can quickly locate the exact file.

5. Tips for Using Advanced Filters Effectively

- **Be Specific**: The more filters you apply, the more precise your search results will be.
- **Start Broad, Then Narrow**: If you're unsure of the file type or date, begin with a general search and add filters progressively.
- **Save Time with Search Shortcuts**: Once you know your search habits, consider saving common queries or using bookmarks in your browser for quick access.

6. Conclusion

Advanced filtering options in OneDrive empower you to take control of your file organization and improve your productivity. By learning how to filter files by type, size, modified date, owner, and shared status, you can locate critical documents, collaborate more effectively, and keep your OneDrive workspace tidy.

Mastering advanced filtering not only saves time but also ensures that you get the most out of your OneDrive experience. So, the next time you need to find a file, don't scroll—filter and discover how effortless file management can be.

CHAPTER III
Sharing and Collaborating

3.1 Sharing Files and Folders

3.1.1 Generating Shareable Links

One of the most powerful features of OneDrive is its ability to easily share files and folders with others using shareable links. Whether you are collaborating on a work document, sharing personal photos, or sending files to clients, creating shareable links provides a quick and convenient solution. In this section, we'll explore what shareable links are, how to generate them, and the different options available for sharing.

What is a Shareable Link?

A **shareable link** is a URL generated by OneDrive that allows others to access your files or folders without needing to sign in to their Microsoft account. These links can be configured with specific permissions, such as allowing someone to view, edit, or download the content.

The primary benefits of using shareable links include:

- **Ease of use**: No complicated processes—just send a simple link.

- **Flexibility**: You can set permissions based on your needs.

- **Accessibility**: Recipients can access files from any device with internet connectivity.

By understanding how to generate and manage these links, you can securely share your files with colleagues, friends, or clients.

Steps to Generate Shareable Links

OneDrive allows you to create shareable links from multiple devices: the web version, the desktop application, and the mobile app. Let's break this down step by step.

A. Generating Shareable Links via the Web Version

The web interface of OneDrive offers a user-friendly way to create shareable links. Follow these steps:

1. **Log in to OneDrive**

   o Open your web browser and go to https://onedrive.live.com.

   o Log in with your Microsoft account credentials.

2. **Locate the File or Folder to Share**

   o Navigate through your folders to find the file or folder you want to share.

3. **Select the Share Option**

   o Hover over the file or folder, and you'll see a checkmark appear. Select it.

   o Click the **Share** button at the top menu or next to the selected file/folder.

4. **Customize Your Link**

   o A pop-up window will appear with sharing options. By default, OneDrive creates a link that anyone with the link can use.

   o To customize permissions, click **"Anyone with the link can edit"**. You can then modify settings:

      ▪ **Allow Editing**: Enable this if you want the recipient to edit the file. Disable it for view-only access.

      ▪ **Set Expiration Date**: Add an expiry date for the link to enhance security.

      ▪ **Set Password**: Protect your link with a password for an extra layer of security.

5. **Copy and Send the Link**

   o Click **Apply** after choosing your desired permissions.

o   Select **Copy Link** and paste it into an email, chat, or messaging app to share with your recipients.

Quick Tip: If you want to send the link directly via email, you can enter the recipient's email address in the "Send Link" section and include a custom message.

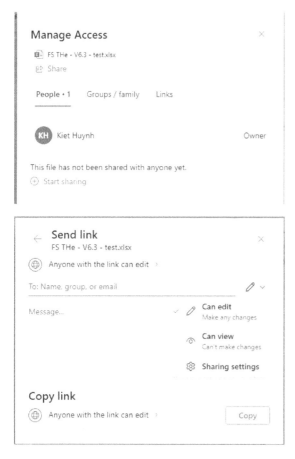

B. Generating Shareable Links via the OneDrive Desktop Application

The OneDrive desktop app integrates seamlessly with Windows File Explorer and macOS Finder, making it easy to create shareable links.

1. **Open File Explorer (Windows) or Finder (Mac)**

   o   Navigate to your OneDrive folder, which is synced to your computer.

2. **Right-Click the File or Folder**

   ○ Right-click on the file or folder you want to share.

   ○ In the context menu, select **Share** or **Share a OneDrive link**.

3. **Choose Link Permissions**

   ○ If you selected **Share**, a pop-up window will appear, similar to the web version. You can customize permissions (view/edit), set passwords, or define expiration dates.

   ○ If you chose **Share a OneDrive link**, a link with default permissions will be copied to your clipboard immediately.

4. **Send the Link**

   ○ Paste the link into an email, chat, or document to share it.

C. Generating Shareable Links on Mobile Devices

Sharing files via the OneDrive mobile app is just as simple. Here's how:

1. **Open the OneDrive App**

   ○ Download and install the OneDrive app if you haven't already.

   ○ Log in with your Microsoft account credentials.

2. **Navigate to Your File or Folder**

   ○ Browse your files to locate the one you wish to share.

3. **Tap the Share Icon**

   ○ Select the file/folder and tap the **Share** icon (usually a square with an arrow pointing up).

4. **Customize Link Settings**

   ○ Choose "Copy Link" to generate a link.

   ○ Tap **Settings** to adjust permissions (view/edit) or add security options like passwords and expiry dates.

5. **Share the Link**

   o Paste the link into a messaging app, email, or SMS to share it with your recipient.

Understanding Link Permissions

When generating a shareable link, OneDrive gives you flexibility to control **how others can interact with your content**. Here are the primary permissions:

1. **Anyone with the Link**

   o This option allows anyone who has the link to access the file/folder, even without signing in.

   o Best for: General sharing of non-sensitive files.

2. **People in Your Organization**

   o Limits access to users within your company or organization.

   o Best for: Sharing internal work documents securely.

3. **Specific People**

   o Restricts access to individuals whose email addresses you specify.

   o Best for: Sharing sensitive or private files.

Best Practices for Generating Shareable Links

To ensure secure and effective file sharing, consider these best practices:

1. **Use Expiration Dates**: For temporary collaborations, set expiry dates on links to prevent unauthorized long-term access.

2. **Restrict Permissions**: Default to view-only access unless editing is absolutely required.

3. **Add Password Protection**: For sensitive files, always enable password protection.

4. **Monitor Access Logs**: Regularly check link usage to ensure no unauthorized access.

5. **Avoid Over-Sharing**: Limit link sharing to only those who truly need it.

Common Use Cases for Shareable Links

- **Team Collaboration**: Share project files and allow team members to edit documents in real-time.

- **Client Deliverables**: Send completed work to clients securely with view-only permissions.

- **Photo Sharing**: Share vacation albums with friends and family via an easily accessible link.

- **File Backups**: Send large files to yourself for backup purposes.

Troubleshooting Shareable Links

If recipients encounter issues with your links, check for the following:

- **Incorrect Permissions**: Verify that the link permissions match the intended access level.

- **Link Expiry**: Confirm that the link has not expired.

- **Recipient Access Issues**: Ensure the recipient's email address is correct (for specific people links).

By mastering the steps to generate shareable links and applying best practices, you can unlock the full power of OneDrive's sharing features. In the next section, we'll explore how to fine-tune permissions and manage access settings to keep your files secure while collaborating effectively.

3.1.2 Setting Permissions

One of the most powerful features of OneDrive is its ability to control exactly who can access your files and what they can do with them. This flexibility is essential for maintaining privacy and security while collaborating with others. In this section, we'll explore the various permission settings available in OneDrive, how to apply them effectively, and practical use cases for each option.

Understanding Permission Levels

When you share a file or folder in OneDrive, you can assign specific permission levels to the recipients. These permissions dictate what actions others can perform with your shared content. Below are the primary permission levels available in OneDrive:

1. **View Only**:

   Recipients can see the file but cannot make changes or download it (if download restrictions are enabled). This is ideal for sharing reports, presentations, or documents that should remain unchanged.

2. **Edit**:
   Recipients can make changes to the file or folder. They can also download and re-share the content unless restricted. This is useful for collaborative projects where multiple people need to contribute or update content.

3. **Full Access**:

   Recipients have the same level of control as you, including the ability to change permissions or delete the file. Be cautious with this option, as it transfers significant control to others.

Setting Permissions When Sharing

When sharing files or folders in OneDrive, permissions can be set during the sharing process. Here's how you can customize these settings based on the method of sharing:

1. Sharing via Links

OneDrive allows you to share files and folders through links. These links can be customized to specify who can access them and what actions they can perform.

- **Steps to Set Permissions for Link Sharing**:

1. Select the file or folder you want to share.

2. Click the "Share" button in the toolbar or right-click and choose "Share."

3. In the sharing dialog box, click on "Copy link" or "Manage access."

4. Customize the link settings:

   - **Who can access**:

     - **Anyone with the link**: The link is open to anyone who has it, with no login required. Use this option cautiously for sensitive files.

     - **People in your organization**: Only individuals within your organization can access the link.

     - **Specific people**: Only individuals you specify can access the link. This option provides the highest level of control.

   - **What they can do**:

     - Allow or block editing.

     - Allow or block downloading of the file.

     - Set expiration dates for the link to automatically revoke access after a certain period.

5. Once settings are configured, click "Apply" and copy the link to share it with recipients.

2. Sharing via Email Invitations

Alternatively, you can send email invitations directly from OneDrive to share content with specific individuals or groups.

- **Steps to Set Permissions for Email Sharing**:

    1. Select the file or folder you want to share and click the "Share" button.

    2. In the sharing dialog box, enter the email addresses of the recipients.

    3. Before sending, click on the "Permissions" dropdown menu to customize access:

        - **Can view**: Recipients can only view the file.

        - **Can edit**: Recipients can view, edit, and download the file.

    4. Optional: Add a personal message explaining the purpose of the shared content.

    5. Click "Send" to share the file or folder.

3. Advanced Permission Options

For more granular control, OneDrive provides advanced permission settings through the "Manage Access" panel:

- **Steps to Use Advanced Permissions**:

    1. Right-click the file or folder and select "Manage Access."

    2. View all active sharing links and recipients.

    3. Click on each link or recipient to adjust individual permissions:

        - Change their access level (View, Edit, or Full Access).

        - Remove their access entirely.

        - Adjust link settings, such as adding a password or expiration date.

    4. Save changes to update permissions immediately.

Practical Scenarios for Permission Management

To better understand how to apply these permission settings, let's explore some practical scenarios:

Scenario 1: Sharing Reports with Clients

A project manager needs to share a financial report with a client but wants to ensure the document remains unaltered. In this case:

- Use the "Anyone with the link" option but disable editing and downloading.

- Set an expiration date for the link to limit access after the project is completed.

Scenario 2: Collaborating on a Team Project

A team leader is working with a group on a presentation. All members need the ability to edit the file and contribute their input. In this case:

- Share the file with "Specific people" and enable editing permissions.

- Allow co-authoring in real-time by using Microsoft Office integration.

Scenario 3: Restricting Access to Sensitive Data

An HR manager needs to share employee performance data with the CEO but wants to keep it private from others. In this case:

- Use the "Specific people" option and share the link directly with the CEO's email address.

- Require a password to open the file for added security.

Tips for Managing Permissions Effectively

1. **Review Permissions Regularly**:

   Over time, files and folders may accumulate a wide range of permissions as you share them with different people. Periodically review these permissions using the "Manage Access" panel to ensure they align with your current needs.

2. **Use Expiration Dates for Temporary Access**:

   For temporary collaborations, always set expiration dates for links. This prevents unauthorized access after the project ends.

3. **Be Selective with "Anyone with the Link"**:

   While this option is convenient, it's also the least secure. Avoid using it for sensitive or confidential files.

4. **Enable Notifications for File Access**:

   Configure your OneDrive settings to receive notifications when someone accesses or edits shared files. This helps you monitor activity and detect potential misuse.

5. **Use Strong Passwords for Protected Links**:

   When sharing highly sensitive information, add an extra layer of security by setting strong passwords for your shareable links.

Common Mistakes to Avoid

- **Granting Too Much Access**:

  Always verify the permissions you grant. For example, don't give editing rights to someone who only needs to view a file.

- **Sharing with Incorrect Recipients**:

  Double-check email addresses and recipient names to avoid sharing sensitive files with the wrong individuals.

- **Overlooking Expiration Dates**:

  Forgetting to set an expiration date can lead to unauthorized long-term access.

By understanding and using OneDrive's permission settings effectively, you can maintain control over your files while enabling seamless collaboration. Whether sharing sensitive business data or working on a team project, OneDrive offers the tools you need to balance security and accessibility.

3.2 Collaborating in Real-Time

3.2.1 Co-Authoring Documents

One of the most powerful features of OneDrive is its ability to enable real-time collaboration on documents. Whether you're working on a report, a presentation, or a spreadsheet, OneDrive's co-authoring capabilities make it possible for multiple users to edit a file simultaneously. This feature eliminates the need for endless email threads, version control nightmares, and repetitive back-and-forth communication. Here, we'll explore how co-authoring works, how to get started, and best practices for a seamless collaborative experience.

What is Co-Authoring?

Co-authoring allows multiple users to work on the same document at the same time, with changes being reflected in real-time. This functionality is integrated with Microsoft Office apps such as Word, Excel, and PowerPoint, both in the desktop and web versions. Co-authoring ensures that everyone involved in a project is always working on the latest version of a document, making it a game-changer for team productivity.

How to Enable Co-Authoring on OneDrive

1. **Upload the Document to OneDrive**

   o To enable co-authoring, the document must first be stored in OneDrive. Upload the file by either dragging and dropping it into a folder in your OneDrive or using the "Upload" button in the interface.

2. **Share the File**

   o Click on the file and select "Share."

   o Generate a shareable link or invite specific collaborators by entering their email addresses.

   o Ensure that you grant "Edit" permissions to enable co-authoring.

3. **Open the File for Editing**

   o   Collaborators can open the file in either the desktop version of the Microsoft Office app or the web-based version in a browser.

   o   Changes made by all collaborators will automatically sync in real-time.

How Does Real-Time Collaboration Work?

When multiple users open the same document in OneDrive, they are immediately notified of each other's presence. Small indicators, such as colored cursors or usernames, show where others are editing in the document. These features foster transparency and allow everyone to stay aware of ongoing changes without confusion.

For example:

- In **Microsoft Word**, you'll see text changes happening live, and a notification will display the name of the person making the edits.

- In **Excel**, cells being edited by others are highlighted in different colors.

- In **PowerPoint**, you can see changes to slides as they are being made, ensuring that designs and content align without conflict.

Benefits of Co-Authoring

1. **Increased Productivity**

   Teams can accomplish tasks faster by working on a single file simultaneously instead of waiting for their turn to make edits.

2. **Transparency and Clarity**

   Real-time visibility into edits and updates helps team members stay aligned and reduces misunderstandings.

3. **Reduced Version Confusion**

   Since everyone is working on the same file, there is no need to reconcile multiple file versions or manually track changes.

4. **Integrated Communication**

Using Microsoft 365 tools, collaborators can leave comments, @mention specific users, or even use Microsoft Teams to discuss the document in parallel.

Best Practices for Co-Authoring

To make the most of OneDrive's co-authoring feature, follow these best practices:

1. **Communicate Roles and Responsibilities**

   o   Assign specific sections or tasks to team members to avoid overlaps.

   o   Use comments and notes to clarify questions or suggestions instead of overwriting others' work.

2. **Leverage Version History**

   o   OneDrive automatically saves previous versions of a document. If something goes wrong, you can restore an earlier version by accessing the "Version History" feature.

3. **Use Comments for Feedback**

   o   Instead of directly altering content, collaborators can leave comments to suggest edits or improvements. This is especially helpful when working on sensitive or high-stakes documents.

4. **Stay Connected**

   o   Pair co-authoring with a communication tool like Microsoft Teams or email to address questions quickly and ensure smooth collaboration.

Troubleshooting Common Issues

1. **Conflicts in Changes**

   o   If two users make conflicting edits to the same section of a document, OneDrive might create separate versions of the file to preserve both sets of changes. These can be manually reconciled later.

2. **Slow Synchronization**

o Ensure that all users have stable internet connections for real-time syncing. Slow or intermittent connections can cause delays in updates appearing for collaborators.

3. **Editing Restrictions**

   o Check permissions for the file. If some users report being unable to edit, confirm that they have "Edit" access rather than "View Only" access.

4. **File Locking**

   o Occasionally, a file may become "locked" if a user opens it in an unsupported app or in offline mode. In such cases, close the file and reopen it using a supported version of Microsoft Office or the web editor.

Practical Example: Team Project Workflow

Imagine a marketing team working on a presentation for a client. With co-authoring in OneDrive:

1. The team leader uploads the PowerPoint file to OneDrive and shares it with the team.

2. The designer begins creating the slide layout, while the content writer drafts key messages simultaneously.

3. The manager reviews the slides, adding comments and feedback using the comment feature.

4. During a live team meeting, everyone can see edits happening in real time, allowing them to finalize the presentation collaboratively.

This seamless process saves time and ensures everyone's contributions are included.

Security Considerations

Co-authoring on OneDrive is secure, with Microsoft's encryption and authentication protocols safeguarding your data. However, it's essential to follow these steps to protect your work:

1. **Review Permissions Regularly**

      ○ Revoke access for collaborators who no longer need it.

2. **Monitor Version History**

      ○ Use the version history feature to track changes and prevent unauthorized modifications.

3. **Avoid Sharing Sensitive Information**

      ○ For confidential documents, consider adding password protection or sharing only with trusted collaborators.

Conclusion

Co-authoring documents in OneDrive revolutionizes how teams collaborate. By enabling real-time edits, fostering transparent communication, and ensuring that everyone works on the same version, this feature boosts productivity and reduces stress. With a little practice and adherence to best practices, teams can unlock the full potential of OneDrive's collaboration tools, making it an essential part of their workflow.

3.2.2 Version History and Changes

One of the standout features of OneDrive is its ability to track and manage version history for files. Whether you're collaborating on a shared document or editing a file on your own, the version history feature ensures that you never lose previous iterations of your work and allows you to recover earlier versions if needed. This section explores the importance of version history, how to access it, and how to make the most of this feature when collaborating in real-time.

The Importance of Version History

When working on shared files, particularly in a collaborative environment, multiple users may contribute changes at the same time. This can lead to situations where edits overlap, critical information is accidentally deleted, or unintended changes disrupt the document's integrity. Version history acts as a safety net, giving users the confidence to experiment and make edits without fear of permanent data loss.

For professionals and students alike, version history is also valuable for tracking progress, revisiting earlier ideas, and understanding how a document has evolved over time. In team settings, it allows members to identify who made specific changes, fostering accountability and transparency.

How to Access Version History

Accessing version history in OneDrive is straightforward and can be done via both the web interface and the desktop application. Follow these steps to view and manage file versions:

Via the OneDrive Web Interface

1. Navigate to your OneDrive account and locate the file you want to review.

2. Right-click on the file and select **Version history** from the context menu.

3. A new pane will appear, displaying all saved versions of the file, along with timestamps and the names of contributors who made the changes.

Via the Desktop Application

1. Open File Explorer (Windows) or Finder (Mac) and locate the file in your OneDrive folder.

2. Right-click on the file and choose **Version history**.

3. A browser window will open, taking you to the version history page for the selected file.

Viewing Changes in Office Applications

If the file is a Microsoft Office document, such as a Word, Excel, or PowerPoint file, you can also view version history directly within the application:

1. Open the file in the respective Office app.

2. Click on **File** > **Info** > **Version history**.

3. A list of previous versions will be displayed on the right-hand side.

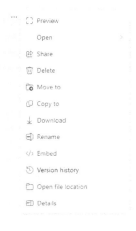

Restoring or Downloading Previous Versions

Version history not only allows you to view past versions but also gives you the option to restore or download them. Here's how:

1. Locate the desired version in the **Version history** pane.

2. To preview the version, click on its timestamp or title. This will open the file in a read-only format.

3. To restore the version, click **Restore**. This will overwrite the current version with the selected one while keeping a record of the replaced version in the history.

4. To download the version as a separate file, click **Download**, allowing you to keep it as a backup or reference.

Use Cases for Version History in Collaboration

Resolving Conflicts

In real-time collaboration, multiple users might simultaneously edit the same section of a document. Version history allows the team to compare edits, identify overlaps, and make decisions on which changes to keep.

Recovering Deleted Information

If a team member accidentally deletes important content, version history provides a quick solution. Instead of manually re-entering the information, you can simply restore an earlier version of the file.

Tracking Contributions

In projects where accountability is essential, version history helps team leaders identify who made specific edits. This is particularly useful in academic or corporate environments where documentation of contributions is required.

Revisiting Past Ideas

Sometimes, an idea or structure from an earlier version of a document may become relevant again. Version history makes it easy to retrieve and incorporate those elements without disrupting the current version.

Best Practices for Using Version History

Encourage Team Awareness

Make sure all collaborators are aware of the version history feature. This reduces hesitation to make changes and provides a sense of security when working on shared files.

Communicate Major Changes

When making significant edits, use the file's commenting or chat features to inform team members. This minimizes confusion and provides context for why certain changes were made.

Regularly Review Versions

In long-term projects, review the version history periodically to track progress and ensure the document remains aligned with team goals.

Name Important Versions

Some files allow you to name or tag specific versions for easier reference later. Use this feature to mark critical milestones or finalized drafts.

Limitations and Tips for Optimal Use

Version Retention Policies

OneDrive's version history retention depends on your subscription plan. For free accounts, version history might only retain a limited number of versions, whereas paid plans typically offer more extensive storage. Be aware of these limitations and download critical versions if necessary.

File Type Support

Version history works best with Microsoft Office files and other compatible formats. For unsupported file types, OneDrive may not track detailed changes, so consider converting them to compatible formats if version tracking is essential.

Integrating with SharePoint

If you're using OneDrive in a business environment with SharePoint, version history becomes even more powerful. SharePoint allows for deeper integration, including advanced workflows and audit logs.

Real-Life Example: Version History in Action

Imagine you're part of a marketing team preparing a presentation for a major client. Throughout the week, team members contribute slides, edit content, and adjust the design. On the day of the meeting, you notice that a critical data chart is missing. Instead of panicking, you use OneDrive's version history to locate the chart from an earlier version of the file. With a few clicks, you restore the chart and finalize the presentation just in time.

Conclusion

Version history is more than just a backup feature; it's a collaboration enabler. By providing a detailed record of changes, OneDrive ensures that teams can work together efficiently while safeguarding their work against accidental errors or overwrites. Mastering this tool will give you confidence when collaborating in real-time and allow you to focus on creativity and productivity without worrying about losing important work.

3.3 Managing Shared Content

3.3.1 Viewing Shared Files

Managing and tracking shared files is a crucial aspect of using OneDrive effectively, especially when dealing with collaborative projects or personal file sharing. OneDrive provides several tools and features that make it easy to view, locate, and manage files and folders that you have shared with others or that others have shared with you. This section explores the methods for viewing shared files, organizing them, and ensuring smooth collaboration.

Understanding the "Shared" Section in OneDrive

OneDrive features a dedicated "Shared" section in its interface, both on the web and mobile apps, which serves as the hub for all shared content. This section is divided into two main views:

- **Shared by You**: This shows all the files and folders you have shared with others, including links you've generated for sharing purposes.

- **Shared with You**: This displays the files and folders that others have shared with you.

These views help you differentiate between files you've sent out versus those you've received, providing clarity in collaborative environments.

Accessing Shared Files on Different Platforms

On the Web Interface

1. **Log in to OneDrive**: Open your browser, go to the OneDrive website, and log in to your Microsoft account.

2. **Navigate to the "Shared" Section**: On the left-hand navigation pane, click on the "Shared" tab.

3. **View "Shared with You"**: This section lists all files and folders others have shared with you.

4. **View "Shared by You"**: Switch to the "Shared by You" tab to see the files and folders you've shared.

Each file entry provides information such as:

- The name of the file or folder.

- The person you shared it with or the person who shared it with you.

- The type of sharing permission (e.g., view-only or edit).

On the Mobile App

1. **Open the OneDrive App**: Launch the app and sign in if necessary.

2. **Access "Shared"**: Tap the "Shared" icon in the bottom menu.

3. **Switch Between Views**: Use the tabs or filters to toggle between files shared with you and files you've shared.

The mobile app also provides quick actions, such as opening shared files, adding them to your offline list, or sharing them further with others.

On the Desktop Client

Although the desktop application doesn't have a specific "Shared" section, files and folders shared with you can often be accessed via links or directly in the web version of OneDrive. Shared files you've added to your OneDrive will also appear in your local folder under their respective directories.

Filtering and Searching Shared Files

When working with a large number of shared files, finding the one you need quickly can be challenging. OneDrive offers several tools to help you locate shared content effectively:

1. **Using the Search Bar**:

   o Enter the name of the file or folder in the search bar at the top of the OneDrive interface.

- o OneDrive will display relevant results, including shared files, based on your query.

- o Use keywords related to the content of the file if you don't remember the exact name.

2. **Applying Filters**:

- o Use filters such as "Shared by" or "Shared date" to narrow down results.

- o These filters can be accessed from the "Shared" section by clicking on the filter icon.

3. **Sorting Options**:

- o Sort shared files by name, date modified, or type for easier browsing.

- o This is especially useful when dealing with multiple shared files from the same individual or team.

Previewing Shared Files

OneDrive allows users to preview files directly within the interface without the need to download or open them in a separate application. This feature supports a variety of file types, including:

- Word documents, Excel spreadsheets, and PowerPoint presentations.

- Images, videos, and PDFs.

To preview a file:

1. Locate the file in the "Shared" section.

2. Click on the file name or tap it if you're using the mobile app.

3. A preview window will open, allowing you to view the content instantly.

Previewing files is particularly useful for quickly checking details without disrupting your workflow.

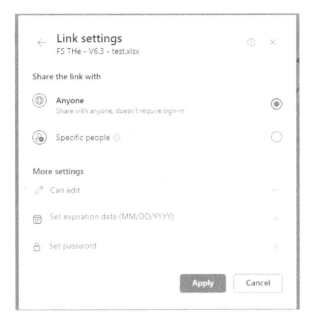

Adding Shared Files to Your OneDrive

For easier access, you can add shared files or folders to your personal OneDrive. Once added, these files will appear alongside your own files, both online and in your synced desktop folder.

1. Locate the shared file or folder in the "Shared with You" section.

2. Click the "Add to My OneDrive" button (available on the web and mobile).

3. The shared file or folder will now be accessible from your primary OneDrive folder structure.

Note: Adding shared files to your OneDrive doesn't transfer ownership; it simply provides quick access while keeping the file linked to the original owner.

Organizing Shared Files

Managing shared files effectively requires organization. OneDrive doesn't allow you to move or rename files directly in the shared folder, but you can use the following strategies:

1. **Create Subfolders in Your Main Drive**:

    o   Add shared files to specific folders in your OneDrive to group them by project, team, or purpose.

2. **Tagging Files in Your System**:

    o   While OneDrive doesn't have a built-in tagging system, you can manually add tags or labels in the file name to make searching easier.

3. **Pinning Important Files**:

    o   Use the "Pin to Quick Access" feature on the web to keep critical files at the top of your "Shared" list.

Best Practices for Viewing Shared Files

- **Regularly Review Shared Content**: Periodically check your "Shared" section to ensure that old or irrelevant files are no longer accessible.

- **Monitor Permissions**: Verify that permissions for shared files align with your collaboration goals. For example, revoke access for users who no longer need it.

- **Communicate with Collaborators**: Use OneDrive comments or integrated Microsoft Teams chats to clarify any issues regarding shared content.

- **Keep a Backup**: For critical shared files, consider creating a backup copy in case the original is deleted by the owner.

Troubleshooting Viewing Issues

Occasionally, you may encounter issues accessing shared files. Common problems include:

- **Expired Links**: If the shared link has expired, request a new link from the file owner.

- **Insufficient Permissions**: If you cannot edit a file you expected to, double-check the permissions with the owner.

- **Sync Issues**: Ensure that shared files added to your OneDrive are syncing properly, especially when accessing them offline.

By following these steps and tips, you'll be able to effectively view, organize, and manage shared files in OneDrive, enhancing both personal and collaborative productivity.

3.3.2 Revoking Access

Sharing files and folders through OneDrive is a powerful way to collaborate with colleagues, family, or friends. However, it is equally important to know how to revoke access when necessary. Whether you no longer want someone to have access, a project has ended, or a link was shared by mistake, understanding how to control permissions ensures your files remain secure and only accessible to those you intend.

This section will explore:

- **When to Revoke Access**

- **How to Revoke Access to Shared Links**

- **How to Stop Sharing Specific Files or Folders**

- **Revoking Access for Individual Users**

- **Monitoring Shared Access**

When to Revoke Access

Knowing when to revoke access is just as critical as sharing files. Below are some common scenarios:

1. **Project Completion**: Once a shared project is finished, you may want to remove collaborators to prevent further edits or accidental changes.

2. **Accidental Sharing**: If you shared a file or folder with the wrong person, revoking access immediately is essential to maintain confidentiality.

3. **Expired Collaboration**: Temporary collaborators, such as contractors or short-term team members, might no longer require access.

4. **Security Concerns**: If you suspect unauthorized access or a security breach, revoking access is a proactive way to regain control.

5. **Permission Updates**: If you want to change a user's access level (e.g., from "Edit" to "View Only"), revoking and re-sharing the file may be the best approach.

How to Revoke Access to Shared Links

OneDrive allows you to share files using links that can be generated for anyone with the link or restricted to specific users. If you need to revoke access, you can stop the link from working entirely or update permissions.

Steps to Remove or Edit a Shared Link:

1. **Access the File in OneDrive**:

   o   Open OneDrive via the web, desktop app, or mobile app.

   o   Navigate to the shared file or folder.

2. **Open the Sharing Settings**:

   o   On the **web**: Right-click the file > Select **Manage Access** or **Share** > **Links Giving Access**.

   o   On the **desktop app**: Right-click the file > **Share** > **Manage Access**.

   o   On the **mobile app**: Tap the file > **Share** > **Manage Access**.

3. **Revoke or Edit the Link**:

   o   To **remove the link completely**: Click the "X" or "Remove Link" button next to the link. Confirm the removal.

   o   To **edit link permissions**: If you don't want to delete the link but need to adjust access (e.g., make it view-only), select **Change Permissions** and update the settings accordingly.

4. **Verify the Change**:

   Once removed, the link will no longer work, and anyone who previously accessed the file via that link will lose access.

Example Scenario:

Imagine you shared a presentation with an external client using a link that grants editing rights. After the project is complete, you decide to stop sharing the file. Simply removing the link ensures that the client can no longer access or edit the presentation.

How to Stop Sharing Specific Files or Folders

When you share a file or folder with others, you can stop sharing it entirely. Revoking access at the file or folder level ensures it is no longer visible to collaborators.

Steps to Stop Sharing a File or Folder:

1. **Locate the File or Folder**:

   o   Open OneDrive and find the file/folder you wish to stop sharing.

2. **Open Manage Access**:

   o   Right-click the file/folder > **Manage Access**.

3. **Stop Sharing**:

   o   On the **web**: Click **Stop Sharing** next to the sharing options.

   o   On the **desktop**: Select the **Sharing** tab, then choose **Stop Sharing**.

   o   On the **mobile app**: Go to **Manage Access** and select **Stop Sharing**.

4. **Confirm the Action**:

   You may see a prompt asking you to confirm the removal of sharing permissions. Confirm, and all shared access will be revoked.

5. **Verify Access Changes**:

   Reopen the file's sharing settings to ensure no links or user permissions remain.

Tip: If you only want to remove sharing for a specific person or group, use the next method to revoke access for individual users.

Revoking Access for Individual Users

If you've shared a file or folder with multiple people and want to revoke access for a specific user without affecting others, follow these steps:

1. **Access Manage Access Settings**:

   ○ Right-click the file/folder > **Manage Access**.

2. **Find the User in the Access List**:

   ○ You'll see a list of users with permissions.

3. **Remove Access for the User**:

   ○ Click the drop-down arrow next to the user's name or email.

   ○ Select **Remove Access** or click the "X" next to their name.

4. **Confirm the Action**:

   Confirm you want to revoke access.

5. **Notify Other Users (Optional)**:

   If necessary, communicate with other collaborators to ensure they are aware of the access change.

Example Scenario:

You shared a team project folder with five team members, but one member leaves the team. Instead of stopping sharing for the entire group, you can individually revoke access for that one user.

Monitoring Shared Access

To maintain control over your shared files, regularly monitor who has access and what permissions they hold.

Steps to Monitor Access:

1. Navigate to the file/folder > **Manage Access**.

2. Review:

   ○ Shared links and their permissions (e.g., "Anyone with the link" or "Specific people").

   ○ Individual users and their roles (View or Edit).

3. Take Action:

   o Revoke, edit, or stop sharing as needed.

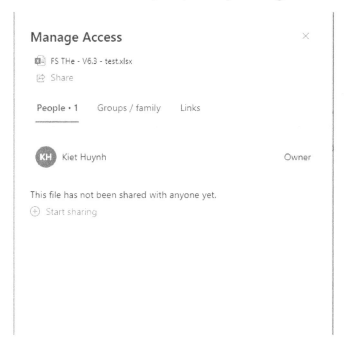

Best Practices for Revoking Access

To efficiently manage shared content and maintain security, consider the following best practices:

- **Regular Reviews**: Periodically review shared files and folders to ensure permissions are up-to-date.

- **Use Expiry Dates**: When sharing files temporarily, set expiration dates for links to automate revocation.

- **Limit Permissions**: Grant "View" access by default, only upgrading to "Edit" when necessary.

- **Audit Collaborators**: Maintain a list of external collaborators and revoke access when they no longer need it.

Conclusion

Revoking access is an essential feature in OneDrive that allows you to maintain control over your files and folders. Whether you need to stop sharing links, remove permissions for specific users, or monitor shared access, the steps outlined above ensure your content remains secure and manageable. By practicing regular reviews and using the tools available, you can confidently share files while keeping your data protected.

CHAPTER IV
Syncing and Offline Access

4.1 Setting Up Syncing

4.1.1 Choosing Folders to Sync

OneDrive sync is an essential feature for users who want seamless access to their files across multiple devices. By syncing specific folders, you ensure that important files are available offline and up-to-date no matter where you are. This feature not only ensures file availability but also makes it easier to work remotely, on the go, or without a constant internet connection. In this section, we'll explore how to select which folders to sync and how to configure OneDrive sync settings to optimize file management.

What Is Syncing and Why Is It Important?

Syncing refers to the process where files or folders are automatically updated across all your devices connected to OneDrive. When you sync a folder, any change made to the files inside it (e.g., editing a document, adding a new file, or deleting one) is reflected across all devices connected to that OneDrive account. This feature is key to managing and accessing files without worrying about the latest version or being online all the time.

Syncing is particularly useful when you work with multiple devices, such as a laptop, desktop, and mobile device. It ensures your files are always available, and it keeps all your devices up to date. You can even set specific folders to sync based on your storage needs and access preferences.

How Does Syncing Work?

When you set up syncing for OneDrive, a folder on your computer becomes linked to the OneDrive cloud storage. Once the folder is synced, any file within that folder is automatically uploaded to the cloud. The OneDrive sync client monitors changes made to the synced folder and updates the files both locally (on your computer) and remotely (on the cloud). This process ensures that the files are always in sync, regardless of where they are accessed.

Choosing Folders to Sync

Selecting which folders to sync is a crucial part of the syncing process. By choosing specific folders, you can ensure that you're not syncing unnecessary data while keeping only the important files available across devices. Here's how to approach folder syncing and make smart choices based on your storage needs:

1. Syncing Entire OneDrive Folder vs. Select Folders

When you first set up OneDrive on your computer, you're given the option to sync everything in your OneDrive account, meaning all files and folders stored on OneDrive will be available on your device. However, syncing everything can take up significant storage space on your device, especially if your OneDrive account contains large files such as videos or high-resolution images.

Instead, OneDrive allows you to choose only specific folders to sync. This can be done through the OneDrive sync settings, and it's a great way to save space while still ensuring that only your essential files are synced. Here's a deeper look at the process of selecting folders:

- **Full Sync**: When you choose to sync your entire OneDrive, all files and folders in your OneDrive account will be stored locally on your device. While this ensures that everything is readily available offline, it can consume a significant amount of storage space. This option is ideal for users with ample storage capacity who want to have everything available at all times.

- **Selective Sync**: With selective sync, you can choose specific folders or files to sync to your computer. This is the preferred method for most users as it helps conserve local storage space. It allows you to choose which files are important and should be available for offline access, while other less crucial files are left in the cloud.

How to Choose Folders to Sync

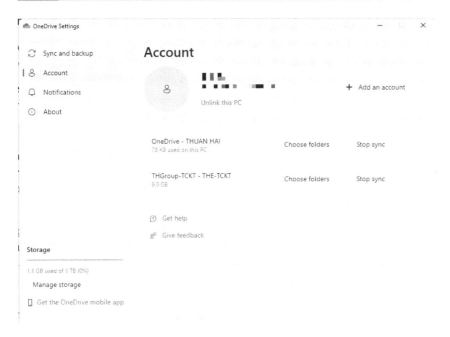

Here's how to configure which folders to sync on your computer:

1. **Open OneDrive Settings**

   o First, click on the **OneDrive icon** in the system tray of your taskbar (Windows) or menu bar (Mac).

   o Click on the **Help & Settings** option (usually represented by three dots or a gear icon) and choose **Settings**.

2. **Access the Account Tab**

   o In the settings window, navigate to the **Account** tab. Here, you will see a section titled **Choose folders**.

   o Click on **Choose folders**, and you will see a list of all the folders in your OneDrive account.

3. **Select Specific Folders to Sync**

   o In the list of folders, you can check or uncheck the boxes next to each folder you want to sync. For example, if you only need access to your "Work" folder, you can uncheck the other folders, such as "Photos" or "Videos," to save space.

o   You can also expand the folders to choose subfolders specifically. This is helpful when you need only a part of a folder synced (e.g., syncing only "Q4 Reports" within a larger "Work" folder).

4.   **Apply the Changes**

o   After selecting the folders you wish to sync, click **OK** or **Apply**. The changes will take effect immediately, and OneDrive will begin syncing only the selected folders.

Considerations When Choosing Folders to Sync

When deciding which folders to sync, keep in mind the following factors:

- **Storage Space**: Choose folders based on how much space they will take up on your device. If you're working with a limited amount of storage, consider syncing only the essential folders that you need immediate access to.

- **Work Priority**: If you have folders containing work-related files, it's a good idea to sync them so they are always available, especially if you work on projects that require real-time updates.

- **Data Sensitivity**: If you have files with sensitive or personal data, you might want to avoid syncing them to certain devices, particularly those that are not secured (e.g., public computers, shared devices).

- **Internet Access**: If you know you will be in locations with limited or no internet access (such as traveling to remote areas), sync the folders that contain files you might need offline.

- **Data Backup**: Syncing important folders ensures that they are backed up in the cloud. However, be selective about which large files you sync to avoid unnecessary backup of media files or older documents that you don't need immediate access to.

Managing Large Folders

If you have large folders that you don't want to sync fully but still need access to, consider syncing them on a case-by-case basis. OneDrive allows users to set up "on-demand" file access, meaning the file or folder stays in the cloud but can be downloaded and accessed whenever needed.

OneDrive **Files On-Demand** is a feature that makes it possible to see and interact with files without downloading them. Files will appear in your OneDrive folder, but they will remain cloud-based unless you manually open them. When you need the file, it is downloaded, and you can work on it offline.

Tips for Managing Folder Syncing

- **Regularly Check Your Sync Settings**: Over time, your folder structure might change, and you may need to revisit your sync settings to ensure you're syncing only what's necessary.

- **Use the Selective Sync Feature to Free Up Space**: If you run low on storage, uncheck large folders or ones that you no longer need access to. This frees up local disk space without deleting the files.

- **Syncing Shared Folders**: If someone shares a folder with you via OneDrive, you can choose whether to sync the shared folder. This is handy for collaborative projects where you don't need every shared folder synced to your device.

Conclusion

Choosing folders to sync in OneDrive is essential for optimizing your device's storage and ensuring that the right files are always available when needed. Whether you choose to sync everything or only select folders, OneDrive gives you flexibility and control. By taking advantage of selective syncing, you can save space while making sure that your essential files are just a click away. In the next section, we will dive into managing sync conflicts, so you can resolve issues that may arise when multiple devices are involved.

4.1.2 Managing Sync Conflicts

When working with cloud-based storage solutions like **OneDrive**, sync conflicts are bound to happen, especially when multiple users access or modify files simultaneously. Sync conflicts occur when OneDrive encounters two or more versions of a file and cannot determine which one to keep. These issues may seem minor at first, but left unchecked, they can lead to lost changes, duplicated files, or disrupted workflows. In this section, we will explore what causes sync conflicts, how to identify them, and strategies to resolve and prevent conflicts efficiently.

What Causes Sync Conflicts?

Sync conflicts in OneDrive typically arise under the following conditions:

1. **Simultaneous Edits:**

   If two people open and edit the same file while offline or using different devices, OneDrive creates conflicting copies because it cannot merge the changes automatically.

2. **Delayed Syncing:**

   When a user makes changes to a file while offline, and another user modifies the same file online, a conflict occurs once the offline user reconnects and OneDrive attempts to sync.

3. **Duplicate File Names:**

   Files uploaded manually to OneDrive with the same name as an existing file can trigger conflicts.

4. **Corrupted Sync Status:**

   Errors in the syncing process, such as an incomplete or interrupted sync, can cause conflicts or duplicates.

5. **Multiple Devices:**

   Users accessing the same OneDrive account across multiple devices may experience conflicts if files are edited on one device but not yet synced to others.

6. **Unresolved Temporary Files:**

   Programs such as Microsoft Office sometimes create temporary files during edits. If these files fail to save or sync correctly, they can trigger conflict issues.

Understanding the root cause of conflicts is critical to managing them effectively and preventing future occurrences.

How to Identify Sync Conflicts

Sync conflicts are easy to identify in OneDrive because the system uses specific indicators to highlight problematic files:

1. **Duplicate File Names with 'Conflicted Copy' Labels:**

When a conflict occurs, OneDrive often saves two versions of the file. It appends one version with the text Conflicted Copy, followed by the name of the user who created the conflict and the date.

Example: AnnualReport.xlsx becomes AnnualReport (Conflicted Copy - John Doe - 01-20-2024).xlsx.

2. **Error Icons in OneDrive:**

   o A **red circle with an 'X' icon** appears next to files that OneDrive cannot sync.

   o The OneDrive taskbar icon on Windows or Mac will also display an error message like, **"OneDrive can't sync this file"** or **"Sync issues detected."**

3. **Conflict Notifications:**

   On some devices, OneDrive provides notifications when conflicts arise, prompting users to take immediate action.

4. **Version History Review:**

   If you are unsure whether a file conflict has occurred, check the **Version History** in OneDrive. Version History allows you to view and compare previous file versions to identify inconsistencies or duplicate edits.

Resolving Sync Conflicts

There are several ways to resolve sync conflicts depending on the nature of the issue and the tools available. Here are step-by-step strategies for managing sync conflicts:

1. Manually Merging Changes

The most common approach to resolving sync conflicts is to manually review and merge changes between conflicting file versions.

- **Step 1:** Identify the two files causing the conflict. Look for the original file and the conflicted copy with the appropriate labels.

- **Step 2:** Open both files and compare the changes. Use tools like Microsoft Word's **Compare Documents** feature to highlight differences.

- **Step 3:** Combine edits into a single file. This may involve copying missing sections from one version to the other or resolving changes line by line.

- **Step 4:** Save the consolidated file and upload it back to OneDrive. Delete the conflicting versions to avoid confusion.

2. Renaming Files to Avoid Conflicts

If you do not need to merge changes, simply rename one of the conflicting versions to preserve both files.

- **Step 1:** Right-click the conflicted file in OneDrive.

- **Step 2:** Choose **Rename** and modify the file name to something unique. For example, rename AnnualReport (Conflicted Copy).xlsx to AnnualReport_John_Edits.xlsx.

- **Step 3:** Sync both files to OneDrive. This resolves the conflict by treating each file as a separate entity.

3. Restoring the Correct Version with Version History

OneDrive's **Version History** feature allows you to recover previous versions of a file without manually resolving conflicts.

- **Step 1:** Right-click the conflicted file in the OneDrive folder (Windows or Mac).

- **Step 2:** Select **Version History** from the menu. A list of previous versions will appear.

- **Step 3:** Review the versions to identify the correct one.

- **Step 4:** Choose **Restore** to overwrite the current file with the desired version.

This option works well when one version of the file clearly contains the correct or most up-to-date changes.

4. Re-Sync the Folder

Sometimes, sync conflicts occur because OneDrive's sync process is interrupted or corrupted. Re-syncing the affected folder can resolve minor conflicts.

- **Step 1:** Pause syncing in OneDrive by right-clicking the OneDrive icon in the taskbar and selecting **Pause Syncing**.

- **Step 2:** Delete the conflicted files locally (ensure backups are available if needed).

- **Step 3:** Resume syncing by selecting **Resume Syncing** in OneDrive. OneDrive will re-sync the folder and download the correct file version from the cloud.

5. Deleting Redundant Conflicted Files

If the conflicted copies contain no valuable information or changes, you can safely delete them.

- **Step 1:** Verify that one version of the file contains the necessary edits.

- **Step 2:** Delete the conflicting copies. Right-click the conflicted file and select **Delete**.

- **Step 3:** Empty the Recycle Bin to permanently remove the redundant files.

Best Practices to Prevent Sync Conflicts

To reduce the likelihood of sync conflicts in the future, consider adopting the following best practices:

1. **Use Real-Time Collaboration Tools:**

   When multiple users need to edit the same document, encourage them to use tools like Microsoft Word's real-time co-authoring feature. This allows changes to sync immediately and prevents conflicting copies.

2. **Stay Online When Editing Files:**

   Avoid making major edits to OneDrive files while offline. If working offline is necessary, notify team members to minimize simultaneous changes.

3. **Regularly Sync Changes:**

Periodically check your OneDrive sync status and ensure all changes are synced across devices. This reduces the chance of unsynced edits causing conflicts.

4. **Communicate with Team Members:**

   In collaborative projects, communicate with others to ensure everyone knows when a file is being edited. Use OneDrive's **Share** feature to assign editing permissions as needed.

5. **Enable File Locking (for Business Users):**

   OneDrive for Business allows users to "lock" files to prevent simultaneous editing.

Conclusion

Managing sync conflicts in OneDrive requires a clear understanding of their causes, careful identification of conflicting files, and deliberate resolution strategies. Whether you choose to merge changes manually, restore previous versions, or re-sync your files, the tools provided by OneDrive ensure that no data is lost in the process. By following best practices like real-time collaboration and proactive communication, you can minimize sync conflicts and enjoy a seamless cloud storage experience.

In the next section, we will discuss **4.2 Accessing Files Offline**, where you'll learn how to enable offline access and ensure your edits sync back seamlessly when you reconnect to the internet.

4.2 Accessing Files Offline

4.2.1 Enabling Offline Mode

Accessing files offline in OneDrive is a crucial feature for users who need their documents, photos, or other files readily available when they don't have access to the internet. Whether you are traveling, working in a remote location, or experiencing an unstable network, enabling **Offline Mode** ensures that your files are accessible and editable anytime.

This section will guide you step-by-step through enabling Offline Mode on various devices, including desktop applications, web browsers, and mobile devices.

1. Understanding Offline Mode

Before diving into the setup, it is important to understand what **Offline Mode** does in OneDrive:

- **Access without Internet**: Offline Mode lets you access and edit files without an active internet connection.

- **Automatic Sync**: Changes made while offline are saved locally and will automatically sync back to the cloud once you regain internet access.

- **File Selection**: You can specify which files or folders you want to make available offline to optimize storage usage.

Enabling offline access ensures that critical files are always within reach. However, users should balance their storage by selecting files that are essential to have offline, especially on devices with limited space.

2. Enabling Offline Mode on Desktop

The OneDrive desktop application provides seamless offline access, allowing users to choose which files or folders to sync. Follow these steps to enable offline access:

Step 1: Launch the OneDrive Desktop App

1. Open the **OneDrive application** on your Windows or Mac computer.

2. Ensure you are signed in with your Microsoft account. If not, enter your credentials to log in.

Step 2: Locate Your Files

1. Open **File Explorer** (Windows) or **Finder** (Mac).

2. In the navigation pane, locate the **OneDrive folder**. This folder displays all your synced files and folders.

Step 3: Mark Files for Offline Access

You have two options for enabling offline access:

- **Option 1: Individual Files or Folders**

  o Right-click on the specific file or folder you want to access offline.

  o Select **"Always keep on this device"** from the context menu.

  o A green checkmark will appear next to the file or folder icon, indicating that it is now available offline.

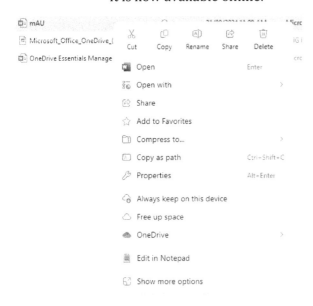

- **Option 2: Selective Sync for Large Folders**

  o Right-click the **OneDrive cloud icon** in your system tray (bottom-right corner on Windows or top menu bar on Mac).

      o   Go to **"Settings"** > **"Account"** > **"Choose folders"**.

      o   Check the folders you need offline access to, then click **"OK"**. These folders will sync locally.

Step 4: Verify Offline Availability

- To ensure your selected files are available offline, disconnect from the internet temporarily.

- Open the file through File Explorer or Finder. If it opens successfully, it has been saved offline.

3. Enabling Offline Mode on Mobile Devices

For those who use OneDrive on smartphones or tablets, offline access is equally straightforward. Here is how to enable offline access on both Android and iOS devices:

Step 1: Open the OneDrive Mobile App

1. Launch the **OneDrive app** on your mobile device.

2. Ensure you are signed in with your Microsoft account.

Step 2: Locate the Files or Folders

1. Browse through your OneDrive folders and locate the file or folder you want to access offline.

Step 3: Enable Offline Access

1. Tap the **three-dot menu** (⋮ or ...) next to the file or folder.

2. Select **"Make Available Offline"** from the menu.

3. A **download icon** (a downward arrow) will appear next to the file or folder, indicating that it is being downloaded for offline access.

Step 4: Managing Offline Files

- To view all offline files:

  - Tap the **"Me"** icon or go to the **Offline Files** section in the OneDrive app. This provides a list of all files available offline.

- To remove offline access:

  - Tap the three-dot menu again and select **"Remove from Offline"**.

4. Enabling Offline Mode on OneDrive for Web

The web version of OneDrive does not inherently support offline access like the desktop app or mobile versions. However, you can achieve similar functionality through browser tools or by using the OneDrive desktop sync app.

Option 1: Use the Desktop Sync App

1. Install the OneDrive desktop application to sync your files locally.

2. Follow the desktop steps to enable offline access.

Option 2: Browser Cache for Temporary Offline Files

Some web browsers, such as Google Chrome, allow you to cache files temporarily for offline viewing:

1. Open the desired file in your browser.

2. Ensure the file is fully loaded.

3. Keep the tab open while offline access is required.

Note: Browser-based offline access is limited and not recommended for long-term offline needs.

5. Managing Offline Storage

Enabling Offline Mode means downloading files locally, which takes up device storage. Managing your storage is essential to ensure your device does not run out of space.

Tips for Managing Offline Files

- **Prioritize Files**: Only enable offline access for files you truly need. Avoid downloading large videos or unnecessary folders.

- **Regular Cleanup**: Periodically review offline files and remove those no longer needed.

- **Monitor Storage Usage**: Check your storage under OneDrive settings to track the space used by offline files.

6. Benefits and Limitations of Offline Mode

Benefits

- Access critical files without internet connectivity.

- Continue working on documents even in remote or offline locations.

- Automatic syncing ensures changes are uploaded when reconnected.

Limitations

- Requires device storage for offline files.

- Files may not sync properly if conflicts arise (covered in **4.1.2 Managing Sync Conflicts**).

- Changes made offline must wait for an internet connection to reflect in the cloud.

7. Troubleshooting Offline Access Issues

Occasionally, offline files may not function as expected. Here are quick troubleshooting tips:

- **File Not Available Offline**: Ensure "Always keep on this device" or "Make Available Offline" is enabled.

- **Storage Full**: Free up device space by removing unused offline files.

- **Sync Delays**: Wait for the files to sync properly before disconnecting from the internet.

Conclusion

Enabling Offline Mode in OneDrive ensures that your files are accessible anytime, anywhere, even without an internet connection. By following the steps provided for desktop, mobile, and limited browser support, you can confidently manage your files offline. Whether for work, school, or personal use, this feature guarantees productivity and convenience, no matter your environment.

In the next section, we'll explore **how to edit offline files and sync them back to the cloud** seamlessly, ensuring your workflow remains uninterrupted.

4.2.2 Editing and Syncing Back Changes

Working offline with your OneDrive files is a practical and efficient feature that ensures you can maintain productivity even when disconnected from the internet. Whether you're on a plane, in a remote location, or dealing with spotty internet access, OneDrive enables you to edit your files seamlessly offline and sync changes back to the cloud when you reconnect. In this section, we will explore how you can edit offline files across various devices, how syncing works once you reconnect, and essential tips for ensuring a smooth workflow.

Understanding How Offline Editing Works

When you enable offline access for specific files or folders in OneDrive, these files are stored locally on your device. This allows you to open, view, and edit them without an internet connection.

Here's how the process works:

1. **Files Are Cached Locally**: OneDrive stores a local copy of your file(s) on your computer, tablet, or smartphone.

2. **Edits Are Recorded**: Any changes you make while offline are saved locally on the device.

3. **Sync Upon Reconnection**: Once your device reconnects to the internet, OneDrive automatically syncs your offline edits to the cloud, updating the version stored on OneDrive.

This seamless process ensures you don't lose any changes and can pick up your work across devices as soon as you're back online.

Editing Offline Files on Different Devices

1. Editing Offline Files on Windows

On a Windows device, editing files offline with OneDrive is simple, as OneDrive integrates directly into the Windows File Explorer.

- **Step 1: Access the File**

  Navigate to the OneDrive folder in File Explorer. Offline-enabled files will appear as **locally available** and can be opened directly with the default program (e.g., Word, Excel, Notepad).

- **Step 2: Edit the File**

  Open the file, make edits, and save as usual. For Office documents, changes are saved automatically if AutoSave is enabled.

- **Step 3: Sync When Online**

  Once your device reconnects to the internet, OneDrive automatically syncs the file. You'll see the **syncing icon** (a circular arrow) appear next to the file. When the sync is complete, the icon will change to a green checkmark.

Pro Tip: Ensure AutoSave is turned on in Microsoft Office applications for smoother edits and faster syncing.

2. Editing Offline Files on macOS

On macOS, OneDrive works similarly to Windows, integrating into Finder for convenient offline access.

- **Step 1: Locate the File**

Open Finder and navigate to the OneDrive folder. Offline files are marked as "Available offline."

- **Step 2: Make Your Edits**

Open and edit the file using the default application, such as Pages, Numbers, or Microsoft Office apps. Save your changes as usual.

- **Step 3: Automatic Sync**

When you reconnect to the internet, the file syncs back to OneDrive. Check the OneDrive icon in the top menu bar to verify sync progress.

3. Editing Offline Files on Mobile Devices

Editing offline files on mobile devices, including iOS and Android, is slightly different due to the mobile app interface.

For Android and iOS Devices:

- **Step 1: Mark the File for Offline Access**

  - Open the OneDrive app.

  - Locate the file you want to access offline.

  - Tap the three dots (...) next to the file name and select **"Make available offline."**

  - The file will download to your device.

- **Step 2: Edit the File**

Use Microsoft Office Mobile apps (Word, Excel, PowerPoint) or other supported apps to open and edit the file.

- **Step 3: Sync Changes**

As soon as you reconnect to the internet, the OneDrive app automatically syncs your edits back to the cloud. A small sync icon next to the file indicates progress.

Note: Offline files take up storage space on your device, so periodically review and remove files no longer needed offline to save space.

How Syncing Back Changes Works

Understanding the syncing process can help ensure your edits are updated correctly when you reconnect to the internet.

1. Automatic Sync Process

OneDrive uses an automatic sync mechanism to detect changes made to offline files. As soon as your device is connected to the internet:

- OneDrive scans all files marked for offline access.

- It identifies files that have been edited locally and syncs these changes to the cloud.

- A new version of the file is created in the cloud (if version history is enabled).

The **sync status icons** in OneDrive can help you monitor this process:

- **Blue circular arrows**: Syncing is in progress.

- **Green checkmark**: Syncing is complete.

- **Red "X"**: An error occurred during syncing.

2. Resolving Sync Conflicts

Sometimes, sync conflicts occur when two versions of a file are edited simultaneously — one offline and the other online. This often happens in collaborative environments.

When a sync conflict arises, OneDrive handles it as follows:

- You'll see a notification in the **OneDrive app** or File Explorer/Finder.

- OneDrive saves both versions of the file:

  o The original file (cloud version).

  o A conflicting file labeled with your device name (e.g., *Document-Conflicted Copy-UserName-PCName*).

To resolve the conflict:

1. Compare both versions of the file.

2. Manually merge changes into one file if necessary.

3. Delete the duplicate/conflicting version once resolved.

---

3. Monitoring Sync Progress

You can monitor sync progress to ensure all offline edits are successfully updated in the cloud:

- **Windows/Mac**:
    - Check the OneDrive icon in the system tray (Windows) or top menu bar (macOS).
    - Clicking the icon shows sync status and any recent activity.

- **Mobile Devices**:
    - Open the OneDrive app and check the sync status under the "Offline" tab or notification center.

Best Practices for Editing Offline Files

Here are some best practices to make the most of offline editing in OneDrive:

1. **Plan Ahead**
    - Before going offline, mark all necessary files for offline access.
    - Test that the files open correctly and edits can be made without an internet connection.

2. **Enable AutoSave**
    - In Office applications, ensure AutoSave is turned on to prevent data loss.

3. **Stay Organized**

- o Keep offline files organized in specific folders to simplify syncing and tracking changes.

4. **Regularly Check Sync Status**

- o After reconnecting to the internet, verify that all changes are synced successfully.

5. **Resolve Conflicts Promptly**

- o Address any sync conflicts as soon as they appear to avoid confusion and data duplication.

6. **Monitor Storage Usage**

- o Offline files consume local storage, so periodically review and clear out files you no longer need.

Troubleshooting Syncing After Offline Edits

If changes are not syncing after you reconnect to the internet, try the following steps:

1. **Check Your Internet Connection**

   Ensure your device has a stable and active internet connection.

2. **Restart OneDrive**

   - o On Windows/Mac: Close and reopen the OneDrive app.

   - o On Mobile: Force stop the app and restart it.

3. **Manually Trigger Sync**

   Right-click the OneDrive icon and select **"Sync now"** to force a manual sync.

4. **Check for Updates**

   Ensure you're using the latest version of the OneDrive app.

5. **Verify Offline Settings**

   Double-check that the file or folder is marked for offline access.

If these steps don't resolve the issue, proceed to reset your OneDrive settings (covered in **Section 4.3.2**).

Conclusion

Editing files offline and syncing changes back to OneDrive is a powerful feature that allows you to work without interruption, regardless of your internet availability. By following the best practices and understanding how the sync process works, you can confidently edit files offline, collaborate with others, and ensure a seamless workflow.

In the next section, we'll discuss common issues that arise during the syncing process and practical solutions to troubleshoot them effectively.

4.3 Troubleshooting Sync Issues

4.3.1 Common Errors and Fixes

Syncing issues are among the most common challenges OneDrive users encounter. While OneDrive is generally reliable, occasional errors can arise due to connectivity issues, settings misconfigurations, or outdated applications. This section outlines the most frequent sync problems users face and provides detailed steps to resolve them effectively.

Error 1: OneDrive Not Syncing at All

Problem:
OneDrive is not syncing any files. The files remain stuck in their previous state, or the syncing process does not start.

Cause:
This issue can arise due to:

- Poor or unstable internet connection.

- OneDrive processes being paused or stuck.

- Application errors or system glitches.

Solution:

1. **Check Your Internet Connection:**

   o Ensure you have a stable and active internet connection. Test it by opening a website or running a speed test.

   o If your connection is slow, try reconnecting or switching to a different network.

2. **Restart OneDrive:**

   o Close the OneDrive app and restart it.

- On **Windows**, click the OneDrive cloud icon in the taskbar > Right-click > **Close OneDrive** > Restart it by searching for "OneDrive" in the Start Menu.

- On **Mac**, click the OneDrive icon in the Menu Bar > Click **Quit OneDrive** > Relaunch it from the Applications folder.

   o This step refreshes the app and clears minor glitches.

3. **Pause and Resume Syncing:**

   o Temporarily pause syncing to reset the connection.

   o To do this:

   - Click the OneDrive icon > Go to **Help & Settings** > **Pause Syncing** > Select a duration (e.g., 2 hours).

   - Wait a few minutes, then click **Resume Syncing**.

4. **Ensure You Are Signed In:**

   o Verify that you are signed in to the correct OneDrive account.

   o Open the OneDrive app and check your login credentials.

5. **Reboot Your Computer:**

   o Restarting your computer resolves temporary system issues that may affect OneDrive.

Error 2: Files Stuck at "Processing Changes"

Problem:
OneDrive displays the message "Processing Changes," and files are not uploading or syncing.

Cause:

- A large number of files are being processed at once.

- One or more files are corrupted or have invalid names.

- Pending updates or system glitches.

Solution:

1. **Check for File Name Issues:**

   o Ensure all file names adhere to OneDrive's naming conventions. Avoid:

      ▪ Special characters like * : " < > ? / |.

      ▪ File paths longer than 400 characters.

   o Rename problematic files and try syncing again.

2. **Stop and Restart the Sync Process:**

   o Pause syncing temporarily, wait for a few minutes, and then resume.

3. **Check for Large Files:**

   o OneDrive has upload limits (e.g., a single file cannot exceed 250 GB).

   o If large files are causing delays, upload them manually using the OneDrive web app.

4. **Clear the OneDrive Cache:**

   o Clearing the cache helps remove stuck or corrupt temporary data.

   o On **Windows**:

      ▪ Open **Command Prompt** and type:

      ▪ %localappdata%\Microsoft\OneDrive\onedrive.exe /reset

      ▪ Press Enter and wait for OneDrive to restart.

   o On **Mac**:

      ▪ Quit OneDrive, then delete the cache folder from Finder:

      ▪ ~/Library/Containers/com.microsoft.OneDrive-mac/Data/Library/Application Support/

Error 3: OneDrive Shows a Red "X" on Files

Problem:

A red "X" icon appears on files, indicating they cannot be synced.

Cause:

- Insufficient storage space.

- File permissions preventing upload.

- Files exceeding size or path limits.

Solution:

1. **Check Your OneDrive Storage Space:**

    o Visit the OneDrive web app to verify your available storage.

    o If you have reached the storage limit, consider:

        ▪ Deleting unnecessary files or folders.

        ▪ Upgrading to a larger storage plan.

2. **Verify File Permissions:**

    o Ensure you have the correct permissions to access or edit the file.

    o Right-click on the file > Properties > Check Permissions.

3. **Fix File Size and Path Issues:**

    o Shorten file paths or folder names if they exceed the allowed length.

    o Ensure no single file exceeds OneDrive's size limit.

4. **Sync the File Manually:**

    o Open the OneDrive app, locate the file with the red "X," and select **Always Keep on This Device**.

    o This forces OneDrive to attempt syncing the file again.

Error 4: "Your OneDrive is Full" Notification

Problem:

OneDrive displays a warning that storage is full even when you believe there's enough space.

Cause:

- Files or folders have not been fully deleted.

- Recycle Bin still contains OneDrive data.

Solution:

1. **Empty the OneDrive Recycle Bin:**

   o Go to the OneDrive web app > Click **Recycle Bin** on the left menu.

   o Permanently delete files from the Recycle Bin to free up space.

2. **Remove Duplicate Files:**

   o Use file management tools to identify and delete duplicates.

3. **Review Large Files:**

   o Identify large files consuming storage using the "Storage Metrics" option in the OneDrive web app.

   o Delete, compress, or transfer these files to another location if necessary.

4. **Upgrade Storage Plan:**

   o If you regularly require more storage, consider upgrading to a paid plan that offers more space.

Error 5: "OneDrive Is Not Connected" Message

Problem:

OneDrive reports it is disconnected, and files are no longer syncing.

Cause:

- Internet connection is lost.

- The OneDrive app is experiencing authentication issues.

Solution:

1. **Verify Internet Connectivity:**

    ○ Ensure your device is connected to the internet. Switch to a different network if needed.

2. **Re-Sign Into OneDrive:**

    ○ Sign out of your account and sign back in:

        ▪ Click the OneDrive icon > Help & Settings > **Settings** > **Account** > **Unlink this PC**.

        ▪ Reconnect your account and restart syncing.

3. **Reset the OneDrive App:**

    ○ Follow the reset steps outlined in **Error 2** to refresh the app and resolve connection issues.

4. **Allow OneDrive Through Firewall or Antivirus:**

    ○ Sometimes, firewall or antivirus software may block OneDrive.

    ○ Add OneDrive to the exception list in your security settings.

By systematically addressing these common errors, you can ensure OneDrive syncs your files seamlessly. If the problems persist, contacting Microsoft Support or reinstalling the OneDrive app may be necessary.

4.3.2 Resetting Sync Settings

Syncing issues can occur in OneDrive for several reasons, including misconfigurations, software glitches, or conflicts with system processes. When other troubleshooting techniques fail to resolve the problem, resetting the OneDrive sync settings is often the best solution. This process restores sync functionality by refreshing your connection to the cloud and clearing any corrupt cache or temporary settings.

In this section, we'll cover:

1. **When You Should Reset Sync Settings**

2. **How to Reset OneDrive Sync Manually**

3. **Using OneDrive Troubleshooter Tools**

4. **Reconfiguring After a Reset**

5. **Best Practices to Avoid Sync Issues After Reset**

When You Should Reset Sync Settings

Before proceeding with a reset, it's essential to confirm whether a reset is the appropriate solution for your problem. Resetting sync will:

- Disconnect your OneDrive account temporarily.

- Clear all cached and temporary sync data.

- Restart the syncing process for your files and folders.

Signs You May Need a Reset:

- Files fail to sync even after restarting the app.

- Sync errors persist despite resolving conflicts manually.

- Files appear stuck on "Processing Changes."

- OneDrive shows duplicate or ghost folders after multiple attempts at fixing issues.

- The app frequently crashes or freezes when syncing large files.

If any of the above symptoms persist, resetting your sync settings is recommended as a clean solution.

Note: Resetting sync settings does not delete your actual files. All files stored in the OneDrive cloud remain safe and accessible after the reset.

How to Reset OneDrive Sync Manually

Depending on your operating system, the process of resetting OneDrive varies slightly. Let's explore step-by-step instructions for both **Windows** and **Mac** users.

Resetting OneDrive on Windows

1. **Close the OneDrive App**

   o   Locate the OneDrive cloud icon in the system tray (bottom-right corner of your taskbar).

   o   Right-click the OneDrive icon and select **Close OneDrive** or **Quit OneDrive**.

   o   If the icon is unresponsive, open the Task Manager by pressing Ctrl + Shift + Esc.

   o   Find **Microsoft OneDrive** under "Processes," right-click it, and select **End Task**.

2. **Run the Reset Command**

   o   Press Win + R to open the Run dialog box.

   o   Type the following command and press **Enter**:

   o   %localappdata%\Microsoft\OneDrive\onedrive.exe /reset

   o   This command resets the OneDrive app by clearing all temporary sync configurations.

3. **Restart OneDrive**

   o   Once the reset process completes, the OneDrive icon will disappear temporarily.

   o   Restart OneDrive manually by opening the Start menu, typing **OneDrive**, and launching the app.

   o   Alternatively, use the Run dialog again and type:

   o   %localappdata%\Microsoft\OneDrive\onedrive.exe

4. **Reconfigure OneDrive Settings**

   o   After restarting, OneDrive will prompt you to sign in again.

   o   Log in with your Microsoft account credentials.

- o Choose the folders you want to sync (as detailed in **4.1.1 Choosing Folders to Sync**).

- o Verify that your files and folders are syncing correctly.

Resetting OneDrive on Mac

1. **Quit OneDrive**

   - o Locate the OneDrive cloud icon in the menu bar (top-right corner).

   - o Click the icon, then select **Settings** > **Quit OneDrive**.

2. **Run the Reset Command**

   - o Open **Finder** and go to **Applications**.

   - o Launch the **Terminal** app (you can search for "Terminal" using Spotlight).

   - o Type the following command and press **Enter**:

   - o /Applications/OneDrive.app/Contents/Resources/ResetOneDriveApp.co mmand

   - o This command resets the OneDrive application.

3. **Restart OneDrive**

   - o Reopen OneDrive from the **Applications** folder or search for "OneDrive" in Spotlight.

   - o Sign in to your Microsoft account when prompted.

4. **Reconfigure Sync Preferences**

   - o Select the folders you want to sync during the setup process.

   - o Ensure files start syncing without errors.

Tip for Mac Users: If resetting fails initially, ensure that the **OneDrive** app has the necessary permissions. Go to **System Preferences** > **Security & Privacy** and grant OneDrive access under **Full Disk Access** and **Files and Folders**.

Using OneDrive Troubleshooter Tools

If manual reset methods don't fully resolve the problem, Microsoft provides additional tools for diagnosing sync issues.

Microsoft Support and Recovery Assistant (Windows)

1. Download the **Microsoft Support and Recovery Assistant** tool from Microsoft's official website.

2. Launch the application and select **OneDrive** from the list of products.

3. Follow the on-screen instructions to scan for and repair sync issues.

4. The tool may reset sync settings as part of the troubleshooting process.

Activity Monitor (Mac)

- If resetting doesn't work, use the **Activity Monitor** to force quit any OneDrive-related processes:

    1. Open **Finder**, go to **Utilities**, and launch **Activity Monitor**.

    2. Search for "OneDrive" under **Processes**.

    3. Select all OneDrive processes and click the **X** icon to quit them.

Reconfiguring After a Reset

After resetting your sync settings, follow these steps to ensure a smooth reconfiguration:

1. **Sign Back into Your OneDrive Account**

    o Launch the OneDrive app and sign in with your Microsoft credentials.

2. **Select Folders for Sync**

    o Use the **Choose Folders** option in OneDrive settings to control which files sync to your device.

3. **Verify Syncing**

    o Check the status of your files by hovering over the OneDrive icon. Look for the message "All files are up to date."

4. **Check for Duplicate Files**

   o A reset may sometimes duplicate certain files or folders. Review your synced folders to ensure no duplicates remain.

Best Practices to Avoid Sync Issues After Reset

Once you've reset OneDrive sync settings, it's important to follow best practices to prevent similar problems in the future.

1. **Keep OneDrive Updated**

   o Regularly update the OneDrive app to ensure you have the latest bug fixes and improvements.

2. **Maintain a Stable Internet Connection**

   o Ensure a reliable Wi-Fi or Ethernet connection during file uploads and sync operations.

3. **Avoid Syncing Large Folders All at Once**

   o Break up large uploads into smaller batches to reduce syncing strain.

4. **Monitor Storage Limits**

   o Check your available OneDrive storage to avoid exceeding limits, which can halt syncing.

5. **Review File and Folder Names**

   o Ensure file names do not contain invalid characters (e.g., <>:"/\|?*) and do not exceed OneDrive's length limits.

6. **Periodically Restart OneDrive**

   o Restart the app occasionally to refresh the connection and clear any minor glitches.

Conclusion

Resetting OneDrive sync settings is a powerful solution to resolve stubborn sync issues. Whether you're a Windows or Mac user, the reset process is straightforward and restores functionality without compromising your files. By reconfiguring your sync preferences carefully and following best practices, you can maintain a smooth and efficient file syncing experience.

If you continue to encounter sync issues after a reset, it may indicate deeper system conflicts or account-related problems, in which case contacting Microsoft Support is the next best step.

CHAPTER V
Advanced Features

5.1 Using OneDrive with Microsoft Office

5.1.1 Saving Directly to OneDrive

OneDrive offers seamless integration with Microsoft Office, providing users with a smooth workflow for saving, accessing, and managing their documents. By using OneDrive, you can ensure that your work is always saved securely in the cloud, accessible from anywhere, and synchronized across your devices. In this section, we'll explore how to save files directly to OneDrive from various Microsoft Office applications, the benefits of doing so, and step-by-step instructions to streamline your document management process.

The Importance of Saving Directly to OneDrive

Saving your work directly to OneDrive has several advantages:

1. **Automatic Cloud Backup**: Files saved to OneDrive are backed up in the cloud, protecting them from loss due to hardware failures or local errors.

2. **Access Anywhere**: Whether you're using a desktop, laptop, tablet, or smartphone, your files are available whenever and wherever you need them.

3. **Collaboration Made Easy**: Files stored on OneDrive can be shared with others for collaboration. Changes can be made simultaneously, ensuring real-time updates.

4. **Version History**: OneDrive maintains a version history for your files, allowing you to revert to earlier versions in case of errors.

5. **Synchronization Across Devices**: When you save to OneDrive, your files are synced across all your connected devices, eliminating the need for manual transfers.

Setting Up OneDrive Integration with Office

Before saving files directly to OneDrive, you need to ensure that OneDrive is integrated with your Microsoft Office applications. Most Office 365 or Microsoft 365 subscriptions already include this integration, but you can follow these steps to verify:

1. **Sign In to OneDrive**: Ensure that you're signed in to OneDrive on your computer and that your OneDrive folder is set up.

   o Open the OneDrive app on your device.

   o Sign in with your Microsoft account credentials.

2. **Verify Your Account in Office Apps**:

   o Open any Microsoft Office application, such as Word, Excel, or PowerPoint.

   o Go to the **File** tab.

   o Select **Account** from the sidebar.

   o Confirm that your OneDrive account is listed under **Connected Services**. If not, click **Add a Service** > **Storage** > **OneDrive** and log in with your credentials.

3. **Set OneDrive as Default Save Location** (Optional):

   o To streamline the process, you can set OneDrive as the default save location for all your documents:

     ▪ Go to **File** > **Options** > **Save**.

     ▪ Under **Save Documents**, check the box for "Save to Computer by default" to turn it off (this prioritizes saving to OneDrive).

Saving Files Directly to OneDrive in Microsoft Word

When you're working in Microsoft Word, saving your documents directly to OneDrive is a straightforward process. Follow these steps:

1. **Starting a New Document**:

   o   Open Microsoft Word and create a new document or open an existing one.

2. **Saving the Document to OneDrive**:

   o   Click the **File** tab to open the backstage view.

   o   Select **Save As** or **Save** if this is your first save.

   o   In the list of save locations, choose **OneDrive**.

       ▪   If your OneDrive account is connected, you'll see your OneDrive folders listed.

       ▪   Navigate to the specific folder where you want to save the document.

   o   Enter a file name and click **Save**.

3. **Quick Save Options**:

   o   Once you've saved the file to OneDrive, you can quickly save changes by pressing **Ctrl + S** (Windows) or **Command + S** (Mac). The changes will be automatically uploaded to OneDrive.

4. **Saving to a Specific OneDrive Folder**:

   o   When saving a file, you can choose any folder within your OneDrive directory. Simply navigate to your desired folder and confirm the save location.

Saving Files Directly to OneDrive in Excel

Excel users can benefit from saving directly to OneDrive to ensure their spreadsheets are secure and accessible. Here's how:

1. **Start a New Workbook**:

   o   Open Microsoft Excel and create a new workbook or open an existing one.

2. **Save to OneDrive**:

   o Click on **File** > **Save As**.

   o Choose **OneDrive** from the list of save locations.

   o Browse your OneDrive folders to select the desired save location.

   o Name your file and click **Save**.

3. **Enabling AutoSave in Excel**:

   o If you're using Office 365, you can enable **AutoSave** to ensure your changes are continuously saved to OneDrive:

     ▪ Look for the **AutoSave** toggle in the top-left corner of the Excel window.

     ▪ Turn it **On**.

     ▪ This ensures that any changes you make are automatically uploaded to OneDrive without the need for manual saving.

Saving Files Directly to OneDrive in PowerPoint

PowerPoint presentations are often shared for collaboration, making OneDrive an ideal storage option. Here's how to save presentations directly to OneDrive:

1. **Create a Presentation**:

   o Open PowerPoint and create a new presentation or open an existing one.

2. **Save the File to OneDrive**:

   o Go to **File** > **Save As**.

   o Select **OneDrive** as the save location.

   o Choose your desired folder, name the file, and click **Save**.

3. **AutoSave for PowerPoint**:

   o Enable **AutoSave** in the same way as in Excel. This ensures your presentation is continuously saved to OneDrive as you work.

4. **Accessing and Editing from Other Devices**:

   o After saving to OneDrive, you can open and edit your PowerPoint presentation from any other device with PowerPoint installed or through the PowerPoint web app.

Saving Office Files from Mobile Devices to OneDrive

Microsoft Office apps, such as Word, Excel, and PowerPoint, are also available on mobile devices, allowing you to save files directly to OneDrive on the go.

1. **Install Microsoft Office Mobile Apps**:

   o Download Word, Excel, or PowerPoint from the App Store (iOS) or Google Play Store (Android).

   o Sign in with your Microsoft account linked to OneDrive.

2. **Saving Files**:

   o Open the app and create or edit a document.

   o Tap the **Save** icon.

   o Choose **OneDrive** as the save location and select the appropriate folder.

3. **Accessing Saved Files**:

   o Once saved, you can access the file from the OneDrive app or any other connected device.

Troubleshooting Common Issues When Saving to OneDrive

If you encounter issues while saving files to OneDrive, here are some solutions:

1. **OneDrive Not Appearing as a Save Option**:

   o Verify that you are signed into OneDrive and that it's connected to your Office applications.

2. **Syncing Issues**:

   o Check your internet connection to ensure OneDrive can sync.

- o Open the OneDrive app and confirm that files are uploading successfully.

3. **File Conflicts**:

- o If multiple users are editing the same document, save your file with a different name to avoid conflicts.

4. **Storage Limits**:

- o If your OneDrive storage is full, delete unused files or upgrade your storage plan.

Conclusion

Saving files directly to OneDrive from Microsoft Office applications provides a powerful and convenient way to manage documents, spreadsheets, and presentations. By leveraging this integration, you can ensure that your files are secure, accessible from anywhere, and easily shareable with collaborators. Whether you're working on a desktop, laptop, or mobile device, OneDrive simplifies the file-saving process, enabling you to focus on your work without worrying about data loss or accessibility issues.

By following the steps outlined in this section, you can take full advantage of OneDrive's capabilities, making your workflow smoother and more efficient.

5.1.2 Accessing Files in Office Apps

OneDrive integrates seamlessly with Microsoft Office applications, offering users a unified experience to access, edit, and save files directly to the cloud. Whether you are using Microsoft Word, Excel, PowerPoint, or Outlook, the convenience of OneDrive enables you to work on documents from any location, on any device, without worrying about losing progress. This section will guide you step-by-step on how to access files stored on OneDrive using various Office applications.

Accessing OneDrive Files from Microsoft Word, Excel, and PowerPoint

When you work with documents in Word, Excel, or PowerPoint, the integration of OneDrive allows you to open, edit, and save files effortlessly. Follow these steps to get started:

1. **Open Microsoft Office Applications**

   o   Launch Word, Excel, or PowerPoint on your desktop, mobile device, or via the web (Office Online). Ensure you are signed in with the same Microsoft account that is linked to your OneDrive.

2. **Navigating the Home Screen**

   o   Upon opening the application, you will see the **Home** screen. Here, you'll find sections such as **Recent Files**, **Pinned Documents**, and an option to **Open** files from various locations.

3. **Accessing Files Stored on OneDrive**

   o   Click on the **Open** tab or go to **File > Open** in the top menu.

   o   You will see several file locations such as:

      ▪   **This PC** (Local Storage)

      ▪   **OneDrive – Personal**

      ▪   **OneDrive – [Your Organization Name]** (for work or school accounts)

   o   Select **OneDrive** to navigate your folders and files stored in the cloud.

4. **Opening a Specific File**

   o   Browse through your OneDrive folders to locate the desired file.

   o   Double-click the file to open it in the application. For Office Online, the file will open directly in the web browser.

5. **Saving Changes Automatically**

   o   One of the most powerful features of working with OneDrive in Office apps is **AutoSave**. Once you open a file from OneDrive, AutoSave is enabled by default, meaning your changes are saved automatically as you type.

   o   To verify that AutoSave is enabled:

- Look for the **AutoSave** toggle in the top-left corner of your Office application window.

- If it is turned off, click the toggle to enable it.

6. **Saving a New Document to OneDrive**

    o If you are working on a new document, follow these steps:

    - Click on **File > Save As**.

    - Select **OneDrive** as the save location.

    - Choose a folder in your OneDrive or create a new folder if needed.

    - Name your document and click **Save**.

Working on Shared Files in Office Apps

OneDrive's collaboration tools extend seamlessly into Office applications, allowing multiple users to work on the same document simultaneously. Here's how you can access and collaborate on shared files:

1. **Accessing Shared Documents**

    o Open Word, Excel, or PowerPoint.

    o Go to **File > Open** and select **Shared with Me**. This section displays all files and folders that others have shared with you.

    o Click on the desired file to open and start editing.

2. **Real-Time Collaboration**

    o Once you open a shared file, you'll see the profile icons of other users who are editing the document. Their changes will appear in real-time.

    o For example, in Word, you can see the cursor position and edits made by other collaborators. Each user's edits are highlighted in a different color.

3. **Adding Comments and Suggestions**

    o Use the **Comments** feature to leave notes for other collaborators. To add a comment:

- Highlight the text or area where you want to leave a comment.

- Go to the **Review** tab and click on **New Comment**.

- Type your comment and press Enter.

o To reply to a comment, click on the comment bubble and type your response.

4. **Version History**

o If you or your collaborators make unwanted changes, OneDrive stores the version history of each document.

o To view previous versions:

- Go to **File > Info**.

- Select **Version History** to see and restore earlier versions of the file.

Accessing OneDrive Files from Outlook

OneDrive integration in Outlook allows you to attach files directly from the cloud instead of uploading them manually. This method saves storage space and ensures recipients always access the latest version of the file.

1. **Attaching Files from OneDrive**

o Open Outlook and create a new email message.

o In the email composition window, click the **Attach File** icon.

o From the dropdown menu, select **Browse Web Locations > OneDrive**.

o Navigate to the desired OneDrive folder and choose the file you want to attach.

o Instead of sending the actual file, Outlook will insert a **OneDrive link**, which allows the recipient to access the file via the cloud.

2. **Setting File Permissions**

- When attaching files via OneDrive, Outlook provides options to set permissions.

- You can choose whether recipients can **View** or **Edit** the file.

- To adjust permissions:

  - Click on the dropdown arrow next to the attachment.

  - Select **Manage Access** to set permissions accordingly.

3. **Accessing Shared Attachments**

- If someone sends you an email with a OneDrive link, click on the link to open the file. It will open in the corresponding Office Online app (Word, Excel, or PowerPoint).

Accessing OneDrive Files on Mobile Office Apps

The Office Mobile apps for iOS and Android also integrate with OneDrive, allowing you to access and work on your files while on the go.

1. **Setting Up OneDrive in Mobile Apps**

- Download the Word, Excel, or PowerPoint app from the App Store or Google Play Store.

- Sign in using your Microsoft account linked to OneDrive.

2. **Opening Files**

- Open the Office app of your choice.

- Tap on **Open > OneDrive**.

- Browse your OneDrive folders and select the file to edit.

3. **Editing and Saving Files**

- Make edits directly within the app. AutoSave is enabled by default, ensuring changes are synced to OneDrive automatically.

4. **Offline Access**

      o   To work offline, mark the file as **Available Offline**. Your changes will sync the next time you connect to the internet.

Benefits of Accessing Files in Office Apps via OneDrive

- **Seamless Integration:** You don't need to upload or download files manually— OneDrive is built into Office apps.

- **AutoSave:** Never worry about losing progress; changes are saved automatically in real-time.

- **Anywhere Access:** Work on your files from any device using the desktop, web, or mobile versions of Office.

- **Collaboration Made Easy:** Access shared files and collaborate with teammates in real time.

- **Version Control:** Easily restore earlier versions of your work with OneDrive's version history.

Conclusion

Accessing OneDrive files directly in Microsoft Office applications is a powerful feature that enhances productivity and collaboration. Whether you're working on your desktop, mobile device, or online, the integration of OneDrive ensures a seamless experience for managing, editing, and sharing documents. By leveraging tools like AutoSave, version history, and real-time collaboration, you can maximize efficiency and stay organized while working in the cloud.

5.2 Integrating OneDrive with Other Tools

5.2.1 Connecting with Teams and SharePoint

OneDrive's integration with Microsoft Teams and SharePoint is a key feature for enhancing collaboration, productivity, and file management across teams and organizations. This section explores how OneDrive seamlessly connects with these tools, providing real-time document access, communication, and effective project management.

What is Microsoft Teams and SharePoint?

Before delving into the connection process, let's briefly define both tools and how they interact with OneDrive:

- **Microsoft Teams:** A collaborative platform combining chat, meetings, file sharing, and task management to facilitate communication and teamwork in businesses and organizations.

- **SharePoint:** A web-based collaboration system used for document sharing, content management, and internal communication. SharePoint works as a central repository for organizational data and enables team members to work on documents collectively.

Both Microsoft Teams and SharePoint integrate directly with OneDrive to create a seamless environment for accessing, managing, and sharing files. While OneDrive focuses on personal file storage, SharePoint and Teams facilitate group collaboration and centralized document libraries.

Why Integrate OneDrive with Teams and SharePoint?

Integrating OneDrive with Teams and SharePoint allows you to:

1. **Centralize Document Storage:** Use SharePoint libraries as team folders to manage shared files while keeping personal work in OneDrive.

2. **Enable Real-Time Collaboration:** Multiple team members can work on documents simultaneously using tools like Word, Excel, or PowerPoint, all synchronized with OneDrive.

3. **Simplify Access:** View and edit SharePoint files directly from your OneDrive interface without navigating between multiple applications.

4. **Enhance Organization:** Group files based on teams, projects, or departments while retaining personal file management in OneDrive.

Connecting OneDrive with Microsoft Teams

OneDrive plays a pivotal role in Teams file sharing. Files uploaded to Microsoft Teams are stored in the backend within SharePoint, while OneDrive integrates for personal or direct chats. Below is a step-by-step guide to connecting and using OneDrive with Microsoft Teams.

1. **Accessing OneDrive Files from Teams**

   o Open **Microsoft Teams** and navigate to the left sidebar.

   o Click on the **Files** tab.

   o Under the Files section, you will see two options: **Microsoft Teams** (team files) and **OneDrive** (personal files).

   o Click on **OneDrive** to view your personal files stored in OneDrive without leaving Teams.

This integration allows you to access your personal cloud files alongside your team documents, streamlining your workflow.

2. **Uploading OneDrive Files to a Teams Channel**

   o Navigate to a **Team** or **Channel** where you want to upload a file.

   o Click on the **Attach** (paperclip) icon in the message bar.

   o Choose **Upload from OneDrive**.

   o Browse through your OneDrive folders and select the file to upload.

o The file will be shared directly in the channel, allowing team members to access and collaborate on it.

Uploaded files will appear under the **Files** tab of the respective channel.

3. **Collaborating on OneDrive Files in Teams**

o When a OneDrive file is shared in Teams, users can click on the file to open it directly in Office Online apps (e.g., Word Online, Excel Online).

o Multiple team members can edit the document simultaneously. All changes are automatically saved and synced back to OneDrive in real-time.

This eliminates the need for attachments or redundant file versions, enhancing team productivity.

4. **Syncing Teams Files to OneDrive Desktop**

o Navigate to a Teams channel and open the **Files** tab.

o Click on **Sync** (available for SharePoint-backed file libraries).

o Teams files will now sync to your OneDrive desktop app, appearing in a folder named **[Your Team/Channel Name]** under the main OneDrive directory.

This allows you to work on Teams documents directly from File Explorer on your computer.

Connecting OneDrive with SharePoint

SharePoint is tightly integrated with OneDrive, serving as the backbone for organizational file storage and team document libraries. SharePoint sites are often associated with Teams channels or specific projects. Here's how to connect and use OneDrive with SharePoint effectively:

1. **Accessing SharePoint Libraries from OneDrive**

o Open the **OneDrive Web Application** or Desktop App.

o Click on the **Shared Libraries** section in the navigation panel.

o All SharePoint sites and libraries you have access to will appear here.

    o   Click on a library to open it and view the files directly in OneDrive.

This connection allows you to manage both personal files (OneDrive) and organizational files (SharePoint) from a single interface.

2. **Syncing SharePoint Libraries to Your Desktop**

    To work offline or access SharePoint files directly in File Explorer:

    o   Open the desired **SharePoint Document Library** in your browser.

    o   Click on the **Sync** button.

    o   A prompt will appear asking you to confirm syncing with OneDrive. Click **Sync Now**.

    o   The SharePoint folder will appear under your OneDrive directory on your computer.

You can now edit, move, and manage files within synced SharePoint folders, and all changes will reflect automatically online.

3. **Saving and Moving Files Between OneDrive and SharePoint**

    o   Open **OneDrive Web App** or **Desktop App**.

    o   Select the file or folder you want to move.

    o   Click **Move To** or **Copy To** and choose the target SharePoint library.

This ensures seamless movement of files between personal storage (OneDrive) and team libraries (SharePoint).

4. **Collaborating on SharePoint Files via OneDrive**

    o   SharePoint files synced to OneDrive can be accessed in Office apps such as Word, Excel, or PowerPoint.

    o   Team members can work on documents simultaneously. Any changes are updated in real-time, ensuring a single source of truth for the document.

5. **Using SharePoint and OneDrive for Version History**

    o   Both SharePoint and OneDrive offer **Version History** to track changes to documents.

- To view previous versions:
  - Right-click on a file in OneDrive or a SharePoint library.
  - Select **Version History**.
  - Restore or view any previous version if necessary.

This feature is invaluable for recovering lost data or reviewing edits made by collaborators.

Tips for Managing Teams and SharePoint Integration with OneDrive

To get the most out of OneDrive's integration with Teams and SharePoint, keep these tips in mind:

1. **Organize Files Strategically:** Use SharePoint for team-wide documents and OneDrive for personal work. Avoid duplication by establishing clear storage policies.

2. **Set Permissions Carefully:** Always review sharing settings before uploading or moving files between OneDrive and SharePoint to prevent unauthorized access.

3. **Sync Regularly:** Sync important SharePoint libraries to your OneDrive desktop app for easy offline access and faster editing.

4. **Leverage Teams for Communication:** Discuss and collaborate on shared files using Teams chats and channels to ensure everyone stays aligned.

Benefits of Integrating OneDrive, Teams, and SharePoint

By connecting OneDrive with Microsoft Teams and SharePoint, users can:

- **Improve Collaboration:** Work seamlessly across personal and team files with real-time updates.

- **Enhance Efficiency:** Access files quickly without switching between platforms.

- **Simplify File Management:** Store, sync, and organize files in a unified environment.

- **Enable Flexibility:** Work offline or online, ensuring productivity from anywhere.

This interconnected ecosystem empowers individuals and teams to streamline workflows, reduce silos, and foster effective communication.

5.2.2 Using OneDrive in Third-Party Apps

OneDrive is more than just a cloud storage solution—it is also a versatile tool that integrates seamlessly with a wide range of third-party applications. These integrations allow you to store, access, and share your files from OneDrive directly within your favorite apps, improving your productivity and streamlining your workflow. This section will explore how to use OneDrive in third-party apps, giving you insights into how to integrate it with tools you might already be using in your daily tasks.

Why Integrate OneDrive with Third-Party Apps?

In today's fast-paced digital landscape, most people use a combination of apps to handle various tasks. From collaboration tools to project management software, the need for seamless integration between cloud storage and third-party tools is growing. By connecting OneDrive with these apps, you can:

- **Access Files Across Multiple Platforms**: With OneDrive integration, you can view and edit your documents from different apps without needing to switch between platforms.

- **Enhance Collaboration**: You can collaborate on documents in real-time, even if you and your team members are using different software.

- **Centralize Your Work**: Using OneDrive across apps allows you to store all your documents and data in one place, reducing the clutter of scattered files.

Let's dive into how you can use OneDrive with some of the most popular third-party apps to unlock its full potential.

1. Integrating OneDrive with Google Workspace

Google Workspace (formerly G Suite) includes popular applications like Google Docs, Google Sheets, and Google Slides. While Google's own cloud storage solution, Google Drive, is commonly used with these tools, integrating OneDrive into the mix can offer additional flexibility, particularly for businesses that already use Microsoft tools.

How to Integrate OneDrive with Google Workspace:

- **Using OneDrive Files in Google Docs/Sheets/Slides**: Google Workspace allows users to link files stored on OneDrive into Google Docs, Sheets, or Slides. This can be done by simply adding a hyperlink to a OneDrive file in a document or using third-party add-ons, like "Google Drive for Office," which enables direct file access from OneDrive.

  - **Steps**:

    1. Open your Google document.

    2. Go to the "Insert" tab and select "Link."

    3. Paste the OneDrive URL of the file you want to share.

    4. Once shared, anyone with the proper access can view or edit the OneDrive file, depending on the permissions set.

- **Using OneDrive as Backup**:

  Many Google Workspace users store important documents on Google Drive. However, if your organization prefers to use OneDrive for backup purposes, you can sync Google Workspace files to OneDrive using third-party sync apps like "CloudHQ." This way, your Google Workspace documents are automatically backed up to OneDrive for additional redundancy.

2. Integrating OneDrive with Slack

Slack is one of the most widely used communication tools in modern workplaces, allowing teams to communicate, share files, and collaborate efficiently. Integrating OneDrive with Slack can enhance your collaboration experience by enabling direct access to your OneDrive files within Slack channels or direct messages.

How to Integrate OneDrive with Slack:

- **Sharing Files from OneDrive**:

  OneDrive can be integrated into Slack through the Slack App Directory, enabling you to share files directly from OneDrive into Slack conversations. This integration lets you search for files stored on OneDrive and share them without having to leave the Slack platform.

- Steps:

    1. Open Slack and go to the "Apps" section.

    2. Search for and install the "OneDrive" app.

    3. Once connected, click the attachment icon in a Slack message.

    4. Select "OneDrive" from the available file sources and choose the file to share.

    5. Slack will automatically add the file to the conversation and notify others of the shared document.

- **Collaborating on OneDrive Files within Slack**:

    After sharing a OneDrive file in Slack, team members can view and collaborate on the document in real-time. This integration ensures that all team members are working with the latest version of the document, improving collaboration and reducing the chances of version control issues.

3. Using OneDrive with Trello

Trello is a popular project management tool that helps teams organize tasks and workflows using boards, lists, and cards. Integrating OneDrive with Trello allows you to attach files from your OneDrive account to Trello cards, streamlining your project management process and ensuring that all important files are easily accessible to your team.

How to Integrate OneDrive with Trello:

- **Attaching Files to Trello Cards**:

    When working on a project in Trello, you can easily attach files stored in OneDrive to your cards. This ensures that your team has immediate access to project-related files directly from the Trello interface.

    - Steps:

        1. Open a Trello card and click on the "Attach File" button.

        2. Select OneDrive as the file source and log into your account.

3. Browse through your OneDrive folders and select the file you wish to attach.

4. The file will appear as an attachment within the card, and team members can download or view it directly from Trello.

- **Real-Time Collaboration on OneDrive Files**:

  By linking OneDrive with Trello, you can also access your documents for real-time collaboration. For example, if you are working on a presentation or spreadsheet related to a specific project, you can edit the file from OneDrive and make live updates visible to all Trello board members.

4. Using OneDrive with Adobe Creative Cloud

Adobe Creative Cloud is a suite of tools used by designers, photographers, and content creators. Integrating OneDrive with Adobe Creative Cloud allows creative professionals to store their work in OneDrive while maintaining easy access to their files in Adobe apps like Photoshop, Illustrator, and Premiere Pro.

How to Integrate OneDrive with Adobe Creative Cloud:

- **Saving Creative Work to OneDrive**:

  You can set up Adobe apps to save projects directly to your OneDrive account. This ensures that your files are backed up to the cloud, providing easy access across different devices, and protecting your work from potential data loss.

  - **Steps**:

    1. Open an Adobe app (e.g., Photoshop).

    2. Go to "File" and select "Save As."

    3. Choose OneDrive as the destination folder.

    4. Your project is now saved to OneDrive, where it can be accessed and edited on any device linked to your OneDrive account.

- **Accessing Creative Files Across Devices**:

By syncing your Adobe files to OneDrive, you can access them from any device with the OneDrive app installed. This feature is particularly useful for creatives who work across multiple locations or devices.

5. Using OneDrive with Zapier for Workflow Automation

Zapier is a powerful tool for automating workflows between different apps. By integrating OneDrive with Zapier, you can create custom workflows that automatically trigger actions in other apps based on changes in your OneDrive files. For example, you can automatically create a new task in Asana when a new file is uploaded to OneDrive or receive a Slack notification when a document is updated.

How to Integrate OneDrive with Zapier:

- **Creating Zaps for File Management**:

  Zaps are automated workflows that link OneDrive with over 3,000 apps. You can create a Zap that automatically saves files from email attachments (such as from Gmail or Outlook) to OneDrive, or trigger an action when a new file is added to a specific folder.

  - **Steps**:

    1. Log into your Zapier account and click "Make a Zap."

    2. Choose OneDrive as the trigger app and select a trigger event (e.g., "New File in Folder").

    3. Choose the app you want to integrate with OneDrive (e.g., Slack, Gmail).

    4. Set the action to take place once the OneDrive trigger is activated.

    5. Test your Zap to ensure it works as expected, then activate it.

Conclusion

Using OneDrive in third-party apps can dramatically improve your workflow by centralizing your files and enhancing collaboration. Whether you're integrating it with Google Workspace, Slack, Trello, Adobe Creative Cloud, or using automation tools like

Zapier, the possibilities are endless. The next step is to start exploring how OneDrive can fit into your existing processes, helping you to be more organized, productive, and efficient.

By taking advantage of OneDrive's integrations, you unlock a powerful ecosystem of tools that work seamlessly together. This makes file management, collaboration, and organization easier than ever, empowering you to focus on what truly matters: getting your work done.

5.3 Automating Tasks with OneDrive

5.3.1 Setting Up Workflows

OneDrive is more than just a cloud storage solution—it also provides powerful tools to automate various file management tasks. Setting up workflows can save time, reduce the risk of manual errors, and enhance your overall productivity by streamlining repetitive tasks. In this section, we will guide you step-by-step through setting up workflows within OneDrive using **Power Automate**—Microsoft's cloud-based automation service.

What Are Workflows in OneDrive?

Workflows are a series of automated steps that trigger actions based on specific conditions or events. For example, a workflow might automatically move a document into a specific folder whenever it is uploaded, or it could send an email notification every time someone shares a file with you. Workflows eliminate the need for manual intervention and allow you to focus on more important tasks.

Microsoft Power Automate, which integrates seamlessly with OneDrive, is the primary tool used to create and manage these workflows. By leveraging pre-built templates or designing custom workflows, you can automate complex processes that would otherwise require manual effort.

Why Use Workflows with OneDrive?

Here are some reasons why setting up workflows with OneDrive can be beneficial:

1. **Increased Productivity**: Automating mundane tasks such as file sorting, moving documents, or sending notifications allows you to focus on more strategic aspects of your work.

2. **Consistency**: With workflows, the same task will be completed consistently every time it's triggered, reducing human error and ensuring your files are managed in an orderly fashion.

3. **Time Savings**: By automating repetitive tasks, you save considerable time and avoid delays in your workflow.

4. **Improved Collaboration**: Workflow automation can streamline collaboration, ensuring that everyone has the right documents at the right time, with no need for manual sharing or tracking.

How to Set Up a Basic Workflow in Power Automate

Before diving into specific workflows, let's walk through how to set up a basic workflow using Power Automate with OneDrive.

Step 1: Access Power Automate

To begin, go to Power Automate, https://make.powerautomate.com/ or you can access it directly from your Office 365 suite. Sign in with your Microsoft account, and you'll be taken to the dashboard where you can manage and create your workflows.

Step 2: Create a New Flow (Workflow)

1. **Select "Create" from the left sidebar**: You will see several options for creating workflows. For this example, choose the **Automated Flow** option. An automated flow is triggered based on an event, such as uploading a file to OneDrive.

2. **Choose a Trigger**: Power Automate will ask you to select a trigger that will start the workflow. You'll be prompted to search for OneDrive triggers. Select the trigger labeled **"When a file is created (properties only)"** or **"When a file is created or modified"**. This trigger will start the workflow when a file is added to a specific OneDrive folder.

3. **Connect to OneDrive**: If you haven't already connected your OneDrive account, Power Automate will prompt you to sign in. Once signed in, you can choose the specific folder within your OneDrive where the workflow will be applied.

Step 3: Define the Action(s)

After setting the trigger, you'll need to define the action that follows. Power Automate gives you multiple options to choose from.

1. **Move Files Automatically**: You can set an action to **move files** into different folders based on certain criteria. For instance, all files with the name "Invoice" could be moved to an "Invoices" folder, while files labeled "Reports" could go into a "Reports" folder. To do this:

   o Choose **Add an Action**.

   o Select the action **Move file**.

- o   Specify the destination folder and any other criteria.

2. **Send Notifications**: Another useful workflow is sending an automatic notification when a file is uploaded or modified. To set this up:

- o   Choose **Add an Action**.

- o   Select **Send an email (V2)** or **Send a push notification**.

- o   Enter the recipient's details and compose the message to notify them about the change or upload.

3. **Update Metadata**: You can also set a workflow to update file metadata based on a condition. For example, if a file is uploaded with a specific keyword in the title, the workflow can automatically update the metadata to reflect the category of the file.

Step 4: Save and Test the Workflow

Once you've configured the trigger and actions, give your flow a name and hit **Save**. You'll be able to test the workflow immediately by uploading or modifying a file in your OneDrive to see if the workflow triggers as expected. Power Automate will notify you if the flow ran successfully or encountered any issues.

Examples of Common Workflows with OneDrive

Now that you know how to set up a basic workflow, here are several practical workflow examples you can set up using Power Automate and OneDrive:

1. **File Organization Workflow**: Automatically move uploaded documents into designated folders based on their file types or names. For instance, you could create a flow that moves PDF files to one folder and Word documents to another.

2. **Daily Backup Workflow**: Set up a workflow that copies important files from one folder to another as a backup every day at a specific time. This ensures that you have the most up-to-date backup of crucial documents.

3. **Approval Workflow for Documents**: When a file is uploaded to a specific folder (e.g., the "Pending Approval" folder), you can set up a workflow to notify a manager or team leader for approval. The manager can approve or reject the file, and the workflow will move the file to either an "Approved" or "Rejected" folder.

4. **Time-sensitive Reminders**: If you work with contracts, deadlines, or documents that have expiration dates, you can create a workflow that sends you a reminder when a file's due date is approaching.

Tips for Optimizing Your Workflows

1. **Use Templates**: Power Automate offers a range of pre-built templates that can save you time in creating common workflows. These templates are customizable and can be tailored to your specific needs.

2. **Set Up Conditional Logic**: You can make your workflows more sophisticated by using conditional logic. For instance, you can set up a flow that only triggers when a file meets certain criteria (e.g., file name, size, or type).

3. **Monitor Workflow Performance**: After setting up your workflows, keep track of how they are performing. You can view the flow's history and troubleshoot any issues that arise. If you notice a workflow isn't behaving as expected, review its steps and make necessary adjustments.

4. **Keep it Simple**: While it's tempting to create complex workflows, remember that simpler is often better. Keep your workflows easy to understand and maintain to avoid unnecessary complications.

Troubleshooting Workflows

Despite its power, Power Automate isn't perfect, and sometimes workflows may not trigger as expected. Here are some tips for troubleshooting:

1. **Check Permissions**: Ensure that you have the necessary permissions to access the files or folders involved in the workflow.

2. **Test and Debug**: Power Automate provides a detailed flow history that can show where the flow may have failed. Use this tool to identify which step in the workflow caused the issue.

3. **Review Conditions and Triggers**: If your workflow isn't triggering, check whether the condition set for the trigger is too specific or if there are issues with the trigger event.

Setting up workflows in OneDrive using Power Automate can significantly enhance your productivity and make managing files easier. By automating repetitive tasks, you reduce the time spent on manual activities and ensure consistency in your file management processes.

5.3.2 Automating File Backups

Introduction to File Backups with OneDrive

Data loss is a common fear for both personal and professional users. Whether it's due to accidental deletion, a system crash, or device failure, losing important files can be catastrophic. OneDrive, as a cloud storage service, offers an effective and convenient way to protect your files through automated backups. By automating file backups to OneDrive, you ensure that your critical data is consistently updated and securely stored in the cloud, minimizing the risks associated with data loss.

In this section, we will explore how to automate file backups using OneDrive. From setting up automatic backups for important folders to leveraging OneDrive's integration with other tools for advanced backup management, this guide will walk you through the essential steps to protect your files without having to worry about manual backups.

Why Automating Backups is Important

Before diving into the steps, it's important to understand why automating backups is so essential:

1. **Convenience:** By automating your backups, you no longer need to remember to perform regular backups. OneDrive will handle this for you in the background.

2. **Protection from Data Loss:** Files that are backed up regularly to OneDrive are protected from device failure, accidental deletion, or corruption. Even if your local storage is damaged, your files are safe in the cloud.

3. **Time-Saving:** Automating backups allows you to focus on other important tasks while OneDrive handles the backup process on your behalf.

4. **Seamless Syncing Across Devices:** With OneDrive, your files are synced automatically across all devices connected to your account. Any new files or changes made on one device will be reflected across all others, keeping your data consistently up-to-date.

Setting Up Automatic Backups on OneDrive

OneDrive offers a few key features to help you automate file backups easily, starting with the "Backup" section, which allows you to select specific folders that will be automatically backed up to your OneDrive account.

1. Enabling Known Folder Move (KFM)

Known Folder Move (KFM) is a simple yet powerful feature that automatically moves and backs up essential folders, such as Documents, Pictures, and Desktop, to OneDrive. This way, you can ensure that these frequently used folders are consistently backed up without having to manually copy files to your OneDrive account.

Here's how to set up Known Folder Move (KFM):

1. **Open OneDrive Settings:** Right-click on the OneDrive icon in the taskbar (system tray) and select **Settings**.

2. **Navigate to the Backup Tab:** In the settings window, click on the **Backup** tab. Here you will find the option to "Manage backup."

3. **Choose Folders to Back Up:** Select the folders you want to back up automatically. Typically, these will be your **Documents**, **Desktop**, and **Pictures** folders. OneDrive will move the contents of these folders to the cloud and ensure that they are continuously backed up.

4. **Enable Backup:** After selecting the folders, click **Start Backup**. OneDrive will automatically begin backing up these folders and syncing them to the cloud. Any changes made to these folders will be reflected across all your devices.

By enabling Known Folder Move, you eliminate the need to manually move files into OneDrive. Any new document, image, or file you create or save to these folders will be backed up automatically.

2. Using OneDrive on Windows 10 and 11 for Folder Synchronization

OneDrive also allows you to automatically synchronize additional folders beyond the default ones. You can select any folder on your PC to sync with OneDrive, ensuring that it's regularly backed up.

To sync custom folders:

1. **Right-click the Folder:** Navigate to the folder on your PC that you wish to sync.

2. **Select "Always keep on this device" or "Free up space":** You can choose to keep the folder stored on your device while also syncing it to OneDrive. This option ensures that files in the selected folder are always available offline, while still being backed up to the cloud.

3. **Check OneDrive Status:** You can check the status of your backups by right-clicking the OneDrive icon and selecting "View sync problems." Here, you'll be able to see if any issues have occurred during the sync process.

This allows you to back up any folder to OneDrive, not just the system folders. For instance, if you have a folder for work documents or project files, you can sync it to OneDrive to ensure it is backed up and accessible from any device.

Using File History for Automatic Backups

File History is a backup feature built into Windows 10 and 11 that allows you to back up files stored on your computer to OneDrive. While OneDrive automatically syncs files in your selected folders, File History offers an extra layer of protection by creating backup copies of your files at regular intervals.

Here's how to set up File History for automatic backups:

1. **Open Settings:** Go to **Settings > Update & Security > Backup**.

2. **Enable File History:** Under the **Back Up Using File History** section, click on **Add a drive** and select your OneDrive as the backup destination.

3. **Choose Backup Settings:** Once OneDrive is selected as your backup location, File History will begin automatically backing up your files at regular intervals. You can customize how often backups occur by clicking on **More Options**.

This option provides continuous protection for your files. In case you need to recover a previous version of a file, you can use File History to easily restore it from the cloud backup.

Automating Backups with Third-Party Apps

While OneDrive offers built-in tools for automating backups, you can also integrate it with third-party backup solutions for more advanced automation features. Many third-party apps offer additional functionality, such as backing up more types of data, automating full disk backups, or scheduling backups at specific times.

Here are a few third-party tools you can use in combination with OneDrive:

1. **SyncBackPro:** This tool allows you to create detailed backup plans, sync files, and schedule backups automatically. SyncBackPro can be set up to back up specific folders to OneDrive at regular intervals.

2. **CloudBerry Backup:** CloudBerry Backup offers more granular control over file backups, including file versioning, backup encryption, and support for multiple

cloud storage providers. You can automate your backup process by setting up scheduled backups to OneDrive.

3. **Acronis True Image:** This full backup solution allows you to back up entire systems or select files to OneDrive. It supports automatic backups at regular intervals and offers features like ransomware protection.

Using third-party apps, you can enhance OneDrive's backup capabilities and make your backup system even more robust.

Best Practices for Automating File Backups with OneDrive

While automating file backups is straightforward with OneDrive, it's important to follow a few best practices to ensure that your files are backed up securely and efficiently.

1. **Set Up Regular Backup Intervals:** Whether you use File History or third-party apps, make sure your backups occur at regular intervals. The more frequently your files are backed up, the less likely you are to lose critical data.

2. **Monitor Backup Status:** Periodically check the status of your backups by accessing OneDrive's sync settings or using third-party apps. If any errors occur, address them promptly to avoid missing backup cycles.

3. **Keep Your Storage Plan in Mind:** OneDrive's free storage plan offers limited space. If you're automating backups of large files or entire folders, ensure that you have enough storage capacity. Consider upgrading to a paid plan if necessary.

4. **Enable Versioning for Important Files:** OneDrive allows you to store multiple versions of a file. This is particularly useful if you need to recover a previous version of a document. Ensure versioning is enabled for important files to have an additional layer of protection.

Conclusion

Automating file backups with OneDrive is an easy yet essential step in protecting your files from data loss. By using features like Known Folder Move, File History, and third-party apps, you can ensure that your data is safely backed up and accessible from anywhere. Automated backups not only save you time but also offer peace of mind knowing that your files are consistently protected in the cloud.

By following the steps outlined in this section, you can automate your file backups with OneDrive and focus on other tasks while OneDrive takes care of keeping your data safe.

CHAPTER VI
Security and Privacy

6.1 Understanding OneDrive Security

6.1.1 Encryption Standards

In today's digital age, security is more important than ever, especially when it comes to storing sensitive information in the cloud. Microsoft OneDrive, like many other cloud storage services, employs a series of encryption methods to protect your data. Encryption is the process of converting data into a coded format to prevent unauthorized access. OneDrive uses encryption to ensure that your files, photos, documents, and other stored content remain private, secure, and protected from unauthorized users.

In this section, we'll explore the encryption standards that OneDrive uses to safeguard your files. We'll also look at how these encryption protocols work to provide a secure environment for your data.

What is Encryption?

Encryption is a cryptographic technique that transforms data from its original readable format (plaintext) into a coded format (ciphertext) using an encryption algorithm and a key. The goal of encryption is to ensure that only authorized parties, such as the file owner or a designated recipient, can read the data.

When data is encrypted, even if an unauthorized party intercepts it, they won't be able to understand or use it because they lack the decryption key required to reverse the encryption process. This provides a strong layer of security for sensitive information.

How Does OneDrive Use Encryption?

OneDrive employs multiple encryption methods to protect your files both in transit and at rest. These two primary methods of encryption are:

1. **Encryption in Transit**

2. **Encryption at Rest**

Let's take a closer look at how each of these works.

Encryption in Transit

When files are uploaded, downloaded, or shared across the network, they are in transit. This is the phase where data is particularly vulnerable, as it travels between your device and Microsoft's data centers. To protect data during transit, OneDrive uses **Transport Layer Security (TLS)** encryption.

Transport Layer Security (TLS)

TLS is the modern version of Secure Sockets Layer (SSL), and it is a protocol designed to ensure secure communication over a network. TLS is widely used across the internet for secure web browsing (HTTPS), email, and file transfers.

OneDrive uses TLS to protect your data while it is being transferred between your device and Microsoft's servers. This means that when you upload or download files from OneDrive, your data is encrypted in transit, preventing eavesdropping or man-in-the-middle attacks, where an unauthorized entity could intercept and alter the data.

Encryption at Rest

Once your files are stored on OneDrive's servers, they are in a state referred to as "rest." Encryption at rest protects your data when it is not being actively used or transmitted. OneDrive employs **AES-256 encryption** to ensure that your files are safe from unauthorized access even if someone manages to gain physical access to the server where your files are stored.

Advanced Encryption Standard (AES-256)

AES-256 is one of the most secure encryption algorithms available today. It is widely used in various sectors, including government and military, for encrypting sensitive information. The "256" in AES-256 refers to the key length used in the encryption process. A longer key length (256 bits) provides stronger security because there are more possible combinations for an attacker to guess, making it exponentially harder to crack.

With AES-256, OneDrive encrypts all files that are uploaded to the platform. Whether you're storing documents, images, videos, or other types of data, they are protected by this high-level encryption standard, ensuring their confidentiality while at rest on OneDrive's servers.

Key Management and Access Controls

OneDrive's encryption is further enhanced by a robust key management system. Encryption keys are used to lock and unlock data, and managing these keys securely is critical to ensuring the overall safety of your files.

Key Management by Microsoft

Microsoft uses a multi-layered approach to key management, where the keys themselves are also encrypted and stored securely. Microsoft ensures that only authorized personnel and systems have access to these keys. Importantly, the encryption keys are stored separately from the data they encrypt, so even if an attacker were to gain access to the storage system, they would still be unable to decrypt the data without the corresponding keys.

Additionally, OneDrive leverages **customer key management** for business and enterprise users. With this feature, businesses can retain control over their encryption keys, allowing them to manage who has access to the encryption keys and monitor their usage. This level of control is particularly valuable for organizations that deal with highly sensitive information and need to comply with strict regulatory standards.

Access Control and Permissions

Encryption alone is not enough to secure your files; access control is equally important. OneDrive allows you to set permissions for individual files and folders. By defining who can view or edit your files, you can add an additional layer of security on top of encryption.

Permissions can be set when sharing files or folders with others, and they can include options such as:

- **View-only access**: Granting someone permission to view the file but not modify it.
- **Edit access**: Allowing someone to make changes to the file.
- **Share restrictions**: Preventing others from sharing the file or folder with others.

These access controls ensure that even if someone gains unauthorized access to your account, they won't be able to view or modify your sensitive files without your permission.

Why is OneDrive's Encryption Important?

The use of encryption in OneDrive is critical for protecting personal, professional, and sensitive data. Here are some of the key reasons why it matters:

1. **Prevent Unauthorized Access**: Encryption ensures that only authorized users can access your files, protecting them from hackers or anyone without the appropriate access rights.

2. **Data Privacy**: Encryption helps maintain the privacy of your data, especially when you are storing personal information such as financial records, medical data, or confidential business documents.

3. **Compliance**: Many industries, such as healthcare, finance, and government, are required to meet strict data protection regulations, such as GDPR, HIPAA, and others. OneDrive's encryption standards help organizations comply with these regulations by providing secure storage options.

4. **Peace of Mind**: Knowing that your data is encrypted both in transit and at rest provides peace of mind. You can trust that OneDrive has implemented robust security measures to protect your files.

The Role of Microsoft's Data Centers

OneDrive operates on Microsoft's cloud infrastructure, which is housed in data centers located across the globe. These data centers are highly secure facilities that have multiple physical and operational safeguards to protect data.

Physical Security

Microsoft's data centers are equipped with multiple layers of physical security, such as surveillance, access controls, and multi-factor authentication (MFA) for personnel entering the facilities. This ensures that even if an attacker were to physically access the data center, they would not be able to tamper with the hardware or data stored on it.

Redundancy and Backup Systems

In addition to encryption, OneDrive's data centers also implement redundancy and backup systems to ensure your data is safe from hardware failures or natural disasters. Redundant power supplies, cooling systems, and network connections ensure that your files are always available and protected.

Conclusion

In summary, OneDrive's encryption standards provide a solid foundation of security to keep your files safe. By employing AES-256 encryption at rest, TLS encryption in transit, and robust key management practices, OneDrive ensures that your data is well-protected from unauthorized access. Additionally, access controls and permission management give you the power to control who can view or edit your files. Whether you are an individual user or part of an enterprise organization, OneDrive's encryption protocols offer peace of mind knowing that your data is secure and private.

As you continue to use OneDrive for file storage and collaboration, understanding these encryption standards will help you make the most of the platform's security features and ensure that your files remain protected in today's digital world.

6.1.2 Two-Factor Authentication

Two-factor authentication (2FA) is one of the most important security features you can enable to protect your OneDrive account. It adds an additional layer of security to your account, making it harder for unauthorized individuals to gain access—even if they have your password. In this section, we will cover what two-factor authentication is, why it's essential for securing your OneDrive account, and how you can enable it to keep your files safe.

What is Two-Factor Authentication?

Two-factor authentication is a security process that requires two separate forms of identification to access an account. This typically involves something you know (like your password) and something you have (like a mobile device or authentication app). By requiring two factors, 2FA significantly reduces the likelihood that a malicious actor can break into your account, even if they have obtained your password through phishing or other attacks.

When enabled on your OneDrive account, you will be prompted to enter your password as usual, followed by a second verification step. This step can come in the form of a code sent to your phone via SMS, an app notification, or even a physical device like a security key. Only someone with access to both your password and the second factor can successfully log in to your account, making unauthorized access much more difficult.

Why is Two-Factor Authentication Important?

1. **Protection Against Password Breaches**

   The most common way that cybercriminals gain access to accounts is by obtaining a user's password. Whether it's through a data breach, phishing attack, or the use of weak, easily guessed passwords, criminals can sometimes steal login credentials. With 2FA, even if a malicious actor has your password, they will still need the second factor to access your account. This extra layer of protection helps prevent unauthorized access and keeps your OneDrive files secure.

2. **Defending Against Phishing and Social Engineering Attacks**

   Phishing attacks have become increasingly sophisticated, with cybercriminals sending fake emails or creating fraudulent websites that trick users into entering their passwords. While 2FA won't prevent these attacks from occurring, it makes it much harder for attackers to use your stolen credentials. Since the attacker would still need access to the second authentication factor (which is often tied to your personal device), they won't be able to log in even with your password.

3. **Mitigating Risks of Weak or Reused Passwords**

   Many users still fall into the trap of using weak passwords or reusing the same password across multiple accounts. In these cases, if a hacker gains access to one of your accounts, they could potentially use the same credentials to access your OneDrive. With 2FA enabled, even if a hacker knows your password, they still need the second authentication factor to get in, greatly reducing the risk of unauthorized access.

4. **Compliance and Regulatory Requirements**

   For businesses and organizations that use OneDrive, enabling two-factor authentication is often a requirement for meeting compliance standards like GDPR, HIPAA, or SOC 2. These regulations require organizations to protect sensitive data with strict security measures, and 2FA helps ensure that your OneDrive account is protected in line with these requirements.

How to Set Up Two-Factor Authentication on OneDrive

Enabling two-factor authentication on OneDrive is a straightforward process, but it requires a few steps to ensure your account is protected properly. Here's a step-by-step guide to help you set up 2FA on your OneDrive account:

Step 1: Sign In to Your Microsoft Account

Since OneDrive is linked to your Microsoft account, the first step is to sign in to your Microsoft account. You can do this by visiting the official Microsoft login page (https://account.microsoft.com) and entering your credentials.

Step 2: Go to Security Settings

Once you've logged in to your Microsoft account, navigate to the "Security" section of the website. You can find this by clicking on your profile icon in the upper-right corner, then selecting "My Microsoft account." From here, select "Security" in the menu.

Step 3: Enable Two-Step Verification

Under the "Security" tab, look for the "Two-step verification" section. You'll be prompted to follow a series of steps to enable 2FA. These steps include:

- **Choosing a Verification Method**: Microsoft offers several ways to receive the second authentication factor, such as via a mobile app (like Microsoft Authenticator), text message (SMS), or email. The most secure method is to use the Microsoft Authenticator app, which generates time-based one-time passcodes (TOTP) for you to use when logging in.

- **Setting Up the Authenticator App**: If you choose to use the Microsoft Authenticator app, download and install it on your mobile device from your device's app store. Once installed, you'll need to follow the on-screen instructions to link the app to your Microsoft account by scanning a QR code.

Step 4: Verify and Confirm

Once you've chosen your verification method, Microsoft will ask you to verify that you have access to the method you selected. If you've chosen to receive a code via SMS, for example, Microsoft will send a test code to your phone. You'll need to enter this code to confirm that you can receive 2FA messages.

Step 5: Backup Options

Microsoft allows you to set up backup methods in case you lose access to your primary authentication method. This could be an additional phone number, an alternate email address, or a printable backup code. It's crucial to set up these options to ensure you can still access your account if you lose your primary device.

Step 6: Complete the Setup

Once all the steps are completed, you will be fully set up with two-factor authentication. Going forward, you will need to enter your password and then provide the second factor each time you sign in to OneDrive.

Types of Two-Factor Authentication Methods

There are several ways to receive your second authentication factor, each with its own pros and cons:

1. **Authentication App (Recommended)**

   Using an authentication app like Microsoft Authenticator, Google Authenticator, or Authy is one of the most secure methods. The app generates a new code every 30 seconds, which you can use to log in. Since the code is generated on your device, it is harder for attackers to intercept compared to SMS codes.

2. **Text Message (SMS)**

   With this method, you receive a code via text message on your phone. While it's easier to set up, SMS is generally considered less secure than authentication apps due to potential vulnerabilities like SIM-swapping, where attackers can take control of your phone number.

3. **Email Verification**

   Some users choose to receive their 2FA code via email. While this is convenient, it's also less secure than other methods, as email accounts can sometimes be compromised.

4. **Hardware Security Key**

   For maximum security, you can use a physical security key, such as a USB device or Bluetooth token. These are plugged into your computer or paired with your mobile device, and they authenticate your login attempts without needing a code.

Managing Two-Factor Authentication

Once 2FA is enabled, it's important to manage your settings and ensure everything remains functional:

- **Review Backup Options**: Make sure your backup authentication options are up to date. If you change your phone number or switch to a new device, update your 2FA settings to reflect these changes.

- **Monitor Login Activity**: Keep an eye on any unusual login attempts. You can view your recent activity through your Microsoft account security dashboard. If you see any suspicious activity, change your password immediately and consider enabling additional security measures.

- **Disable 2FA When Necessary**: If you ever need to temporarily disable two-factor authentication, you can do so through your account settings. However, we recommend only doing this if absolutely necessary, as it will leave your account more vulnerable.

Conclusion

Two-factor authentication is a simple yet powerful way to enhance the security of your OneDrive account. By requiring both your password and a second factor, such as a code from your mobile device or a security key, you can significantly reduce the risk of unauthorized access. Enabling 2FA is one of the most effective steps you can take to protect your personal and professional files stored on OneDrive. Take the time to enable two-factor authentication today and ensure that your files remain secure from potential threats.

6.2 Managing Privacy Settings

Managing privacy settings is an essential part of using OneDrive securely and effectively, especially when it comes to sharing files and collaborating with others. One of the key elements of managing your privacy is configuring account permissions. By understanding and setting appropriate permissions, you can ensure that your data is accessible to the right people and protected from unauthorized access.

6.2.1 Configuring Account Permissions

When you store files in OneDrive, you are often sharing them with others or working on collaborative projects. OneDrive gives you control over how files are shared and who can view or edit them. Account permissions allow you to restrict or grant access to your files, ensuring that only the right individuals have access to sensitive information.

Understanding Permissions in OneDrive

Permissions in OneDrive are linked to how files and folders are shared. There are three main types of permissions you can configure:

1. **View Permissions**: This permission allows the user to only view a file or folder. They cannot make any changes to the document, upload, or delete files within the folder.

2. **Edit Permissions**: With edit permissions, a user can view, add, modify, or delete files in a folder. This is ideal for collaboration scenarios where multiple people need to update a document or contribute files to a shared folder.

3. **Owner Permissions**: The owner of the file or folder has full control over it. The owner can change permissions for other users, delete the file or folder, and perform any other action that the file allows.

When sharing a file or folder, you'll be able to choose from these options. You should always ensure that permissions are granted based on the user's role or level of involvement in the shared project. For instance, give edit access to collaborators working together on the same document but only view access to those who need to read the file without making any changes.

Sharing Files and Folders with Specific Permissions

In OneDrive, the process of sharing files or folders begins with selecting the item you want to share. Here's a detailed guide on how to configure account permissions:

1. **Select the File or Folder**

   To share a file or folder, begin by navigating to the item in your OneDrive directory. Right-click on the file or folder and select the "Share" option. Alternatively, you can select the item and click on the "Share" button from the toolbar.

2. **Choose Sharing Options**

   After clicking "Share," a dialog box will appear where you can configure the sharing settings. You will be given several options, including the ability to share with specific people, anyone with the link, or people in your organization.

   - **Specific People**: This option ensures that only the people you specify can access the file or folder. You will need to enter their email addresses, and they will receive an invitation with a link to the file.

   - **Anyone with the Link**: When you choose this option, the link to the file or folder can be accessed by anyone who has it. However, you can also set expiration dates for the link or require a password to access the content.

   - **People in Your Organization**: This allows anyone in your organization to access the content but requires them to log in using their organizational credentials.

3. **Set Permissions**

   Once you have chosen who can access the file, you will be prompted to select the type of permissions they should have. You can toggle between **Can Edit** and **Can View** to specify whether the recipients can make changes or just view the content.

4. **Send the Invitation**

After selecting the appropriate permissions, you can add a message if needed, and then click "Send" to share the file or folder with the designated recipients. They will receive an email with a link to access the shared item.

Managing Permissions for Existing Shares

Once files and folders are shared, you can manage and modify permissions at any time. This is useful when the collaboration changes, or if you need to restrict or expand access.

1. **View Who Has Access**

   To check who has access to a shared item, simply right-click the file or folder and select "Manage Access" from the options. This will show a list of people who have been granted access and their respective permission levels.

2. **Changing Permissions**

   If you want to change the permissions for an existing user, click on their name and select whether you want to switch from **Can Edit** to **Can View** or vice versa. For stricter control, you can revoke access entirely by clicking on the "Stop Sharing" button for that user.

3. **Adding or Removing People**

   You can also add new people to the share by clicking on the "Add People" button in the "Manage Access" section. To remove someone, click on the "X" next to their name in the list.

Permission Settings for Shared Folders

Managing permissions for folders in OneDrive follows a similar process as managing individual files, but there are additional features to consider:

1. **Folder Permissions vs. Individual File Permissions**

   When sharing a folder, all files within the folder inherit the permissions set for the folder. However, you can modify permissions for specific files within the folder without changing the folder permissions. To do so, right-click the file and choose "Manage Access."

2. **Allowing Others to Share**

OneDrive also lets you configure whether people with access can share the folder or file with others. You can control this by toggling the "Allow editing" option, which determines if users with access can further share or modify the content.

3. **Subfolder Permissions**

For subfolders, OneDrive typically follows the same permission model as the parent folder. However, you have the option to configure subfolders with different permissions from the parent folder, allowing you to grant different levels of access based on the project or team involved.

Collaborating on Files with Different Permission Levels

When collaborating on files, it's important to assign permissions in a way that supports workflow without compromising security. Here are a few tips for collaborative environments:

- **Use View-Only Permissions for Sensitive Documents**

  For files that contain sensitive information, such as financial reports or confidential contracts, restrict access to view-only permissions. This will prevent others from accidentally or intentionally modifying the document.

- **Allow Editing for Collaborative Projects**

  In cases where multiple team members need to work on the same document, grant them edit permissions. This ensures that everyone can make contributions and changes to the document in real-time, such as when creating a joint presentation or drafting a report.

- **Version Control**

  To track changes and avoid accidental overwrites, enable version control. OneDrive automatically saves versions of your files so you can easily restore previous versions if necessary. It's useful to regularly review the version history, especially in collaborative settings, to ensure that edits are tracked.

Best Practices for Configuring Permissions

1. **Regularly Review Permissions**

Over time, you may find that some files or folders no longer need to be shared. Periodically review the access permissions and revoke access for users who no longer need it. This helps maintain a secure environment and reduces the risk of unauthorized access.

2. **Use OneDrive Groups for Simplified Sharing**

If you often collaborate with the same group of people, consider using Microsoft 365 Groups or SharePoint Teams. By creating a group, you can simplify permission management. Members of the group will automatically receive the appropriate permissions for any shared folders or files.

3. **Set Expiry Dates for Links**

If you're sharing files temporarily or for a short-term project, consider setting an expiration date for the link. This automatically revokes access once the time frame has passed, ensuring that the file is not accessible indefinitely.

4. **Apply Permissions Based on Roles**

When sharing files in a team environment, assign permissions based on roles. For example, project managers may need edit permissions to update documents, while team members may only require view access.

By configuring account permissions carefully and consistently, you can ensure that your OneDrive account remains secure and your shared content is properly managed. This helps maintain privacy while promoting effective collaboration and communication across teams.

6.2.2 Monitoring Access Logs

In today's digital age, security and privacy are paramount. OneDrive, as a cloud storage solution, provides various tools to ensure that your files are safe, both in terms of unauthorized access and monitoring any suspicious activity. Monitoring access logs is a powerful feature that can help you understand who has been accessing your files and when, ensuring that you remain in control of your data.

Access logs in OneDrive give users the ability to track file activity, providing a detailed view of who accessed specific files, what actions they took, and when these actions occurred. Whether you're using OneDrive for personal storage or within a business context, being able to monitor access is essential to maintaining privacy, compliance, and security.

What are Access Logs?

Access logs are records that detail activities related to files and folders in your OneDrive account. These logs capture key actions such as file views, edits, downloads, and shares. They also track who performed these actions, the timestamp of when the actions were carried out, and the device or application used. Monitoring these logs helps you quickly identify unauthorized or suspicious activity, track team collaboration, and ensure compliance with internal data management policies.

OneDrive provides access logs primarily for business and enterprise users. However, personal users can also get limited visibility into file activity via version history and sharing logs. In this section, we will discuss how you can leverage access logs in OneDrive to strengthen your security posture and ensure that your files are being used appropriately.

Why Monitor Access Logs?

1. **Track File Access**: The most obvious reason to monitor access logs is to see who is accessing your files. You may want to ensure that only authorized individuals are viewing or editing your sensitive files. For example, if you have a document containing personal or confidential information, knowing who has opened it and when can give you peace of mind.

2. **Detect Suspicious Activity**: Monitoring access logs enables you to spot unusual activity that could indicate a security breach. If a file that is typically accessed by a small group of individuals is suddenly accessed by someone unfamiliar, or if there is a high frequency of access from an unfamiliar location, these are red flags that warrant further investigation.

3. **Ensure Compliance**: For business users, ensuring compliance with legal, regulatory, and internal data governance standards is critical. Access logs allow administrators to verify that employees or collaborators are following the correct processes when handling sensitive data. For example, in industries like healthcare, finance, and legal services, tracking access to sensitive information is required by law, and OneDrive provides a way to capture this data.

4. **File Collaboration**: If you're collaborating on shared files with multiple users, access logs help you track who has made changes to a file, ensuring that everyone is working on the correct version. It also lets you see if any user has accidentally deleted or altered important documents.

How to Access and Review OneDrive Access Logs

Access to detailed access logs is available mainly for OneDrive for Business or SharePoint users. Here's how to access and review these logs in OneDrive for Business:

1. **Sign In to OneDrive for Business**: Begin by logging into your OneDrive for Business account via the web interface at onedrive.live.com or via the OneDrive app.

2. **Access the Admin Center**: If you are an administrator, you can access OneDrive activity logs through the Microsoft 365 Admin Center. To do this, navigate to the Admin Center and select "Security & Compliance." From here, you can review activity logs, including file access, sharing activities, and more.

3. **Use the Microsoft Purview (Compliance) Portal**: For more detailed information about user activity, including file accesses and edits, you can use the Microsoft Purview compliance portal. This portal provides a range of auditing and reporting features for admins to monitor access to files, folders, and SharePoint sites.

4. **Search the Activity Report**: If you're a regular user (non-admin), you can still check basic file activity via the OneDrive app or web interface. In OneDrive, right-click on a file or folder, and select "Details" to see recent activity. For shared files, you can also see a log of who has accessed, edited, or shared the file in question.

5. **Generate Activity Reports**: For more thorough auditing, administrators can generate detailed activity reports in the Admin Center. These reports include information about who accessed files, when they accessed them, what actions were taken (view, edit, download), and the IP address or device used for the access.

Key Types of Access to Monitor

1. **File View**: This log entry tells you when a file was opened by a user. While simply viewing a file may not seem alarming, repeated views of a document that should only be accessed by a limited audience can indicate potential security concerns. If

a file is being accessed outside of the normal schedule or by users who shouldn't have access, this should be flagged.

2. **File Edits**: Monitoring who edits a document is crucial, especially when files are shared or collaboratively worked on. Knowing who made changes to a file and when can help you verify if someone has altered it incorrectly, or if collaboration is proceeding as planned. Edits to important files should be monitored closely to ensure data integrity.

3. **File Downloads**: Downloading files is another significant action that should be tracked. This is particularly important if you're dealing with sensitive or private data. Unauthorized downloads of files, especially by users who do not need to access certain documents, can indicate potential data exfiltration. Monitoring this activity helps prevent unauthorized access to important files.

4. **File Sharing**: Sharing logs show you who shared files and with whom. If a file is shared outside of the intended circle of people, you may want to investigate further. Monitoring shared links and permissions will help you avoid unintended exposure of private or confidential files.

Interpreting the Access Logs

Once you have access to the logs, it's important to know how to interpret them effectively. Look for the following:

- **Frequent Access**: If a file or folder is being accessed more frequently than normal, it may indicate that someone is regularly working on it. However, if it's a file you're not familiar with or it contains sensitive data, this could be a cause for concern.

- **Access from Unknown Devices or Locations**: Files accessed from a device or location that doesn't match typical usage patterns should raise a red flag. If a file is opened from an unknown IP address or a geographical location that seems out of the ordinary, it could be a sign of unauthorized access.

- **Permissions Changes**: Pay attention to any modifications to permissions. If the permissions of a document change—especially from restricted to open access—this could be a potential security breach.

Best Practices for Monitoring Access Logs

1. **Regularly Review Logs**: Regular monitoring of access logs is the best way to stay on top of file activity. You can set up automated alerts for specific activities, such as file downloads or edits, so you're notified if something unusual occurs.

2. **Set up Alerts**: Use alerts to keep track of activities that require immediate attention. For example, if someone tries to access a file they don't have permission to view, you can set up an alert to notify you. Likewise, you can get alerts for suspicious login attempts, repeated failed password attempts, or changes to file-sharing settings.

3. **Audit Logs for Compliance**: For businesses, conducting periodic audits of access logs is vital for compliance purposes. These audits help ensure that your team is following organizational protocols and regulations.

4. **Enable Retention Policies**: To ensure that you always have access to logs for auditing purposes, enable retention policies that specify how long logs should be kept. This is essential for businesses in regulated industries that need to maintain detailed records of file access for extended periods.

Conclusion

Monitoring access logs is an essential practice to maintain the security and privacy of your OneDrive files. By regularly reviewing these logs, setting up alerts, and interpreting file activity, you can ensure that your data is protected from unauthorized access and potential breaches. Understanding who is accessing your files, when they are being accessed, and what actions are being taken provides a clear picture of the security of your data. Whether you're using OneDrive for personal or business use, incorporating access log monitoring into your security routine is a key step towards safeguarding your files and maintaining privacy.

6.3 Best Practices for File Security

6.3.1 Creating Strong Passwords

In the modern digital world, passwords are the first line of defense for your personal and business data. Creating a strong password is essential for ensuring the security of your OneDrive account and the sensitive information stored within it. A weak password is an open invitation to cybercriminals, who can use various methods like brute force attacks or phishing to gain unauthorized access to your data. This section provides detailed guidance on how to create strong, secure passwords that will help protect your OneDrive files.

The Importance of Strong Passwords

Before diving into the specifics of how to create strong passwords, it's crucial to understand why they are so important. Your password acts as the key to your digital world—granting access to your files, emails, and personal information. If your password is easily guessed or weak, hackers can exploit vulnerabilities in your accounts, leading to data theft, identity theft, or financial loss. In the context of OneDrive, a compromised password could expose sensitive documents, financial records, or personal data, making it a prime target for malicious actors.

With cyber threats becoming more sophisticated, using weak or default passwords is no longer an option. As cybercriminals continue to develop new techniques to crack passwords, it's crucial to stay one step ahead by using strong, unique passwords that are hard to guess or hack.

Characteristics of a Strong Password

A strong password is one that is difficult to guess or crack using automated methods. Here are some key characteristics that make a password strong:

1. **Length**: The longer the password, the harder it is to crack. A strong password should be at least 12 characters long. Longer passwords are more resistant to brute-force attacks, where a hacker attempts to guess the password by trying every possible combination.

2. **Complexity**: A strong password should contain a mix of different characters, including uppercase and lowercase letters, numbers, and special characters. This diversity in character types increases the number of possible combinations, making it more difficult for hackers to guess your password.

3. **Unpredictability**: Avoid using common words, phrases, or easily guessable information such as your name, birthdate, or "password123." Passwords that rely on dictionary words or personal details are easier for attackers to guess, especially using a technique known as "dictionary attacks."

4. **Uniqueness**: Never reuse passwords across multiple accounts. If one account is compromised, all accounts with the same password are at risk. Creating unique passwords for each account ensures that even if one password is exposed, the rest of your online presence remains secure.

Techniques for Creating Strong Passwords

Now that you understand the key characteristics of a strong password, here are several techniques you can use to create your own:

1. Use a Passphrase

A passphrase is a longer string of words that is easier for you to remember but difficult for attackers to guess. Instead of using a single word, consider creating a passphrase made up of four or more random words. For example, "BlueTiger$MoonDance&42." This passphrase is long, includes a mix of characters, and is not easily guessable.

To make a passphrase even stronger, try incorporating a combination of unrelated words, numbers, and special characters. Avoid using common phrases or quotes from books, movies, or songs.

2. Incorporate Randomness

You can create a truly random password by using a random password generator. Many password managers, such as LastPass or Dashlane, have built-in generators that create random passwords for you. These passwords are typically a string of letters, numbers, and symbols that have no apparent pattern or meaning, making them incredibly difficult to guess or crack.

For example, a password generated randomly might look like "9w$8R@3tX6!pLz2." While this is not easy to remember, using a password manager can help store and retrieve this complex password securely.

3. Leverage Acronyms

Another method to create a strong password is by using acronyms or abbreviations. Think of a sentence or phrase that is meaningful to you, and then take the first letter of each word to form an acronym. For example, the sentence "I love hiking in the mountains on Sundays" could become "Ilh1nTMo$." This method results in a password that is long, unpredictable, and personal to you.

4. Use Keyboard Patterns (But Avoid Simple Ones)

Some people opt for keyboard patterns, like "Qwerty123" or "12345678." While this may seem easy to remember, these are extremely common and easily guessed by hackers. However, you can use more complex keyboard patterns that are harder to guess. For example, "z2@4M1+eF7!" combines a keyboard pattern with numbers and symbols, creating a more secure password.

5. Avoid Personal Information

One of the most common mistakes people make when creating passwords is using personal information like names, birthdays, or phone numbers. Although these may be easy for you to remember, they are also easy for hackers to find through social media or public records. Avoid using such personal details in your passwords.

Instead, focus on random combinations of characters that don't relate to your personal life or any easily accessible information about you. The more random the password, the harder it will be for attackers to crack.

Tools for Managing and Creating Strong Passwords

Creating and managing strong passwords can be a challenge, especially if you have multiple accounts. Fortunately, there are several tools available that can help you create, store, and manage strong passwords securely.

1. Password Managers

Password managers are applications that store and encrypt your passwords. They can generate strong, unique passwords for each account and autofill login details, so you don't have to remember them. Some popular password managers include:

- **LastPass**: Offers a free version that includes password storage, a password generator, and secure sharing.

- **Dashlane**: Provides a password manager with a built-in password generator and additional security features like dark web monitoring.

- **1Password**: Allows you to store passwords, credit card information, and other sensitive data securely.

Using a password manager eliminates the need to memorize every password and ensures that your passwords are long, complex, and unique for each account.

2. Two-Factor Authentication (2FA)

While not directly related to creating passwords, enabling Two-Factor Authentication (2FA) adds an extra layer of security to your OneDrive account. Even if your password is compromised, 2FA ensures that a hacker cannot access your account without the second form of authentication (usually a code sent to your phone or email).

Most password managers and online services, including OneDrive, support 2FA, and it's highly recommended to enable it for additional protection.

Tips for Maintaining Password Security

Once you've created strong passwords, it's important to maintain their security over time. Here are some tips to help you do so:

1. **Change Passwords Regularly**: While it's not necessary to change passwords frequently unless there's a security breach, it's a good practice to update your passwords every 3-6 months. This ensures that your accounts stay secure in case a password has been exposed without your knowledge.

2. **Don't Share Passwords**: Avoid sharing your passwords with others unless absolutely necessary. If you need to share access to a file or folder, OneDrive allows you to share links and set permissions instead of sharing your password.

3. **Monitor Your Accounts**: Regularly review the devices and locations where your OneDrive account is logged in. If you notice any unfamiliar activity, change your password immediately and enable 2FA for additional security.

4. **Use Unique Passwords for Critical Accounts**: For accounts that hold particularly sensitive information (like your OneDrive account), always use the strongest password possible. These accounts should be treated with extra caution.

Conclusion

Creating strong passwords is one of the simplest and most effective ways to protect your OneDrive files and personal data. By following the techniques outlined in this section— using long, complex, and unique passwords, and employing password managers—you can significantly enhance the security of your accounts. Coupled with other security measures, such as Two-Factor Authentication, strong passwords form the foundation of a robust digital security strategy.

6.3.2 Avoiding Phishing Attacks

Phishing attacks are a widespread threat in the digital world, and cloud services like OneDrive are not immune to these types of attacks. Phishing is a deceptive technique used by cybercriminals to trick individuals into divulging sensitive information such as passwords, financial details, or personal information by impersonating trustworthy entities. In the context of OneDrive, phishing could lead to unauthorized access to your files, loss of data, or worse—identity theft. Understanding how to avoid phishing attacks and take proactive steps to safeguard your information is essential.

This section will guide you through the most common types of phishing attacks, how to recognize them, and the best practices you can adopt to protect your OneDrive account and files from malicious actors.

What Is Phishing?

Phishing is a form of cyber attack that typically involves fraudulent emails, websites, or text messages designed to mimic legitimate sources, such as Microsoft, OneDrive, or other well-known companies. The goal of phishing is to persuade the recipient to click on a link, download an attachment, or enter personal details into a fake form. Once the attacker gains access to the information, they can use it for malicious purposes, including identity theft, unauthorized access to your accounts, and financial fraud.

Phishing attacks can take several forms, including:

- **Email Phishing:** This is the most common form, where the attacker sends an email that appears to come from a legitimate company or service, such as Microsoft or OneDrive. The email may contain a link that directs you to a fraudulent login page designed to steal your login credentials.

- **Spear Phishing:** Unlike general phishing, spear phishing is a more targeted attack where the hacker customizes the email to make it look more credible. The attacker might use information about your organization, colleagues, or personal preferences to make the message appear legitimate.

- **Smishing and Vishing:** Smishing uses text messages (SMS) to trick victims into clicking a link or providing sensitive data, while vishing involves phone calls or voice messages. These types of phishing are increasingly common and often take advantage of urgency, such as claiming your account will be locked unless you respond immediately.

Recognizing Phishing Attacks

The first step in avoiding phishing attacks is learning how to recognize the signs of a phishing attempt. There are several red flags to watch for in phishing emails and other forms of communication:

1. **Suspicious Email Addresses:** Phishing emails may come from email addresses that look similar to legitimate ones but have slight differences. For example, an email may appear to be from Microsoft, but the address may be something like "microsoft-support@onlivemail.com" instead of "microsoft.com."

2. **Urgency or Threats:** Phishing emails often create a sense of urgency or fear to push you into acting quickly. Common tactics include messages like "Your account has been compromised—click here to reset your password" or "Failure to act

immediately will result in account suspension." Legitimate companies like Microsoft would not send such aggressive warnings.

3. **Suspicious Links:** Phishing emails often include links that direct you to fraudulent websites. To spot these, hover your mouse pointer over any link in the email. If the URL looks unfamiliar or does not match the official website's address (e.g., "microsoft.com"), it's likely a phishing attempt. Always verify the URL before clicking.

4. **Requests for Personal Information:** Legitimate companies, including Microsoft, will never ask for sensitive information like passwords or credit card details via email. If an email or message requests this kind of data, it is a clear sign of phishing.

5. **Spelling and Grammar Errors:** Phishing emails often contain grammatical mistakes, poor punctuation, or awkward language. Professional companies typically take care to proofread their communications before sending them out.

6. **Unsolicited Attachments:** Be wary of email attachments, especially if they come from unknown senders. Opening attachments can trigger the download of malware that can compromise your files and personal information.

How to Protect Yourself from Phishing Attacks

While phishing attacks can be convincing, there are several strategies and practices you can adopt to protect yourself and your OneDrive account from these threats.

1. **Enable Two-Factor Authentication (2FA):** As discussed earlier in this chapter, enabling Two-Factor Authentication (2FA) is one of the most effective ways to secure your OneDrive account. Even if a hacker obtains your password through a phishing attack, they would still need access to your secondary authentication method (such as a text message or authenticator app) to gain entry.

2. **Verify Links and Websites:** Always verify the authenticity of any link or website you're asked to visit. If you receive an email claiming to be from Microsoft OneDrive, don't click on the link right away. Instead, open a new browser window and type in the official OneDrive website address (onedrive.com) to log in. This ensures you are going to the correct website.

3. **Educate Yourself and Others:** Awareness is one of the best defenses against phishing. Stay informed about the latest phishing scams and share this knowledge with others in your organization or family. The more people are aware of phishing tactics, the less likely they are to fall victim to them.

4. **Use Anti-Phishing Tools:** Most modern browsers and email clients, such as Microsoft Outlook, include anti-phishing features that automatically flag suspicious emails and websites. Ensure that these features are enabled on your devices. Additionally, you can use third-party security software that offers advanced phishing detection and protection.

5. **Regularly Update Your Passwords:** Changing your passwords regularly is a simple but effective way to protect yourself. Make sure your passwords are complex—use a combination of letters, numbers, and special characters—and avoid reusing the same password across multiple accounts.

6. **Look for HTTPS in the URL:** When accessing your OneDrive account or other sensitive services online, always ensure the website starts with "https://" (not just "http://"). The "s" stands for secure, meaning the connection is encrypted, making it harder for attackers to intercept your information.

7. **Report Suspicious Activity:** If you receive a suspicious email or message that appears to be a phishing attempt, report it to Microsoft. Most companies, including Microsoft, have dedicated phishing report channels. By reporting these incidents, you help protect others and contribute to the ongoing effort to stop phishing attacks.

8. **Use a Password Manager:** Password managers are tools that securely store and manage your passwords. They can help you generate strong passwords for each of your accounts and automatically fill them in when you log in. Using a password manager eliminates the temptation to reuse passwords or write them down insecurely.

9. **Avoid Using Public Wi-Fi for Sensitive Transactions:** Public Wi-Fi networks are more vulnerable to attacks, and cybercriminals can easily intercept sensitive data transmitted over these networks. Avoid logging into your OneDrive account or making any sensitive transactions over public Wi-Fi. If you must use public Wi-Fi, use a Virtual Private Network (VPN) to secure your connection.

Conclusion

Phishing attacks are a significant threat to your online security, but by staying vigilant, following best practices, and using the right tools, you can protect yourself and your files stored in OneDrive. Remember to always question the legitimacy of unsolicited communications, and when in doubt, take the extra step to verify the sender or website before clicking any links or sharing personal information.

By incorporating these security habits into your daily routine, you ensure that your OneDrive account remains safe from malicious actors, allowing you to use the cloud storage service with peace of mind.

CHAPTER VII
Troubleshooting and FAQs

7.1 Common Issues and Solutions

OneDrive is generally a reliable and user-friendly cloud storage solution, but like any software, users may encounter occasional issues. This section will walk you through some of the most common problems and their solutions, specifically focusing on login issues and file syncing errors. By understanding how to troubleshoot and resolve these issues, you can ensure smooth usage of OneDrive.

7.1.1 Login Problems

Understanding the Problem

Login issues are one of the most frequent problems that users face when using OneDrive. This can be frustrating, as it prevents access to your files and folders, and can stop you from syncing data across devices. There are several possible reasons why you may experience login problems, including incorrect credentials, connectivity issues, account configuration errors, or even a OneDrive server outage. Here's how to address these issues.

1. Incorrect Username or Password

One of the simplest reasons you might encounter login issues is using the wrong credentials. It's easy to forget your username or password, especially if you have multiple Microsoft accounts or use a password manager. Here's how to fix this issue:

- **Check Your Username**: Make sure you are using the correct Microsoft account email address. OneDrive uses your Microsoft account to sign in, so your email address needs to be valid.

- o **Tip**: If you're not sure which email address is linked to your OneDrive account, check the email account you typically use for your Microsoft services like Outlook, Office, or Skype.

- **Reset Your Password**: If you can't remember your password or if it's not working, go to the Microsoft password reset page. You'll be prompted to enter your email address and follow the instructions to reset your password.

  - o **Tip**: If you use two-factor authentication, make sure you have access to the method you set up (phone number or authentication app) to receive the verification code.

- **Check Caps Lock and Keyboard Layout**: It's easy to overlook these settings when entering your password. Make sure the Caps Lock key is off and that you are using the correct keyboard layout.

- **Use the Correct Sign-in Method**: If you're using a school or work account, verify that you're signing in with the correct method. Some organizations require specific authentication processes, such as signing in through a company portal or using multi-factor authentication (MFA).

2. Account Lock or Suspended Account

Another reason for login issues is when your account is locked or suspended. Microsoft may lock your account temporarily for security reasons or if suspicious activity is detected. Here's how to resolve it:

- **Unlock Your Account**: If you receive a message saying your account is locked, follow the steps on the Microsoft account recovery page https://account.live.com/acsr to unlock it. This may involve verifying your identity by entering a code sent to your phone or email.

- **Account Suspended**: If your account is suspended due to billing issues or a violation of Microsoft's terms of service, you'll need to resolve the underlying issue. Visit the Microsoft account recovery page https://account.microsoft.com/ for more details on how to reactivate your account.

- **Check for Office 365 or OneDrive Subscription Issues**: If you are using a paid version of OneDrive through Office 365 or Microsoft 365, ensure your subscription is up to date. Sometimes, login problems arise because of expired or inactive subscriptions. Visit the Microsoft subscription management page https://account.microsoft.com/ to review your plan and make any necessary payments.

3. Connectivity Issues

Another common issue that can cause login problems is connectivity. If you're unable to log into OneDrive, it may be due to a weak or intermittent internet connection. Here's how to troubleshoot connectivity issues:

- **Check Your Internet Connection**: Ensure your device is connected to a stable internet network. Try browsing other websites or apps to verify the internet connection is active. If possible, switch to a more reliable Wi-Fi network or use an Ethernet connection for more stability.

- **Disable VPN**: If you are using a VPN (Virtual Private Network), it could be interfering with your login. Try disconnecting from the VPN and attempt to log in again. Some VPNs block access to Microsoft services like OneDrive.

- **Check Firewall and Antivirus Settings**: Sometimes, firewalls or antivirus software can block your connection to OneDrive's servers. Ensure that OneDrive is allowed through your firewall by checking your security software settings.

- **Clear Browser Cache and Cookies**: If you're accessing OneDrive via a browser and facing login problems, clearing your browser's cache and cookies can often resolve issues related to old or corrupted data. Navigate to your browser's settings and clear the cache and cookies, then try logging in again.

4. Server or Service Outage

Occasionally, OneDrive's servers may experience temporary outages or disruptions, which can prevent users from logging in. If you're certain your credentials and connection are correct, the issue might lie with Microsoft's servers.

- **Check Microsoft Service Status**: To see if there's an ongoing issue with OneDrive or other Microsoft services, visit the Microsoft Service Health Status https://status.cloud.microsoft/ page. If there's a widespread outage, Microsoft will typically notify users, and you may need to wait until the issue is resolved.

- **Contact Microsoft Support**: If you have confirmed that the issue isn't on your end, and the Microsoft service status page doesn't indicate any outages, you may need to contact Microsoft Support for further assistance. They can help you determine if there's an issue specific to your account or region.

5. Two-Factor Authentication (2FA) Issues

If you've enabled two-factor authentication (2FA) for your Microsoft account, you may face login issues if there's a problem with receiving the authentication code. Here's how to resolve this:

- **Verify 2FA Method**: Ensure that your 2FA settings are up to date and that you can access the authentication method (phone number, email, or authentication app). If you're using an app like Microsoft Authenticator, ensure it is properly synced with your account.

- **Use Backup Codes**: If you're unable to receive the authentication code, Microsoft provides backup codes during the 2FA setup process. Use these codes to log in when you don't have access to your primary 2FA method.

- **Disable 2FA Temporarily**: If all else fails and you need to access your account urgently, you can temporarily disable two-factor authentication through your Microsoft account security settings, though this should be a last resort for security reasons.

7.1.2 File Syncing Errors

OneDrive is designed to make file synchronization seamless across all your devices. However, syncing errors can occasionally occur, causing confusion and frustration for users. Understanding why syncing errors happen and how to troubleshoot them is crucial to maintaining a smooth workflow and ensuring your files remain up to date across all platforms. In this section, we'll dive deep into common syncing errors and offer solutions to help you resolve them quickly and effectively.

Understanding OneDrive Syncing

Before we address specific errors, let's first understand how OneDrive syncing works. OneDrive syncs files between your devices and the cloud, ensuring that the most recent version of a file is available no matter where you access it. This syncing process is typically automatic, but for various reasons, it may fail or become interrupted.

The OneDrive sync client checks the status of the files stored locally on your device and in the cloud. It then syncs any changes made to the files on one device to all other connected devices. However, when syncing errors occur, these changes may not be reflected, leading to out-of-date files or incomplete file uploads.

Common Causes of Syncing Errors

Several factors can contribute to syncing errors in OneDrive. Let's explore some of the most common ones:

1. **Internet Connectivity Issues**

   One of the primary causes of syncing errors is poor or intermittent internet connectivity. Since OneDrive relies on an active internet connection to sync files between your devices and the cloud, a slow or unstable connection can cause syncing failures. You may see an error message indicating that OneDrive cannot connect to the cloud or sync files.

2. **Outdated OneDrive Client**

   Using an outdated version of the OneDrive sync client can lead to various issues, including syncing errors. OneDrive is regularly updated with new features and bug fixes. If your sync client is outdated, it may not work correctly, causing issues like files failing to upload or sync across devices.

3. **File and Folder Name Issues**

   File and folder names that contain special characters, such as *, ?, <, >, or |, can cause syncing problems. OneDrive is designed to work with most characters, but certain characters are not supported for file names in the cloud. If you attempt to upload a file or folder with unsupported characters, the syncing process may fail, or the file may be ignored.

4. **File Size and Storage Limits**

   OneDrive offers a set storage limit for both individual files and your overall account. If you are attempting to upload a file that exceeds the maximum file size limit or if your account storage has reached its capacity, syncing errors will occur. You might see an error message indicating that the file cannot be uploaded or synced.

5. **Corrupted Files**

   Occasionally, a file may become corrupted due to improper closing, system crashes, or issues during upload. Corrupted files cannot sync properly, and OneDrive will either fail to upload them or display an error message.

6. **Conflicting File Versions**

If a file is being edited simultaneously on multiple devices, syncing conflicts can occur. OneDrive might create duplicate files, or it may fail to sync the correct version, leading to discrepancies in your files. Conflicting versions can occur if changes were made offline and not synced properly when reconnecting to the internet.

7. **Insufficient Permissions**

If you do not have the proper permissions to access a file or folder, syncing errors can occur. For example, if you have been granted view-only permissions for a file, you may not be able to sync any changes made to it. Similarly, if you lack permission to access a folder, files inside that folder may not sync.

8. **Device-Specific Issues**

Sometimes, syncing errors may be specific to a particular device. For example, a file may sync fine on your desktop but not on your laptop due to a conflict or issue specific to that device, such as system settings, software conflicts, or problems with your OneDrive app installation.

How to Resolve File Syncing Errors

Now that we understand the common causes of syncing errors, let's explore practical solutions to fix these issues.

1. Check Your Internet Connection

If you're experiencing syncing issues, start by checking your internet connection. Ensure that you are connected to a reliable Wi-Fi network or have access to a stable mobile data connection. If your internet connection is slow or unstable, try restarting your router or switching to a different network.

Solution:

- Check if other devices on your network are experiencing similar issues, which could indicate a problem with the network itself.

- Try moving closer to your Wi-Fi router or resetting your router.

- If you're using a mobile device, switch to a stronger Wi-Fi signal if possible.

2. Update Your OneDrive Client

An outdated OneDrive client may be causing syncing errors. To ensure that OneDrive works smoothly, make sure you're using the latest version of the client. Updating OneDrive ensures that any known bugs or glitches are fixed, and you gain access to new features and improvements.

Solution:

- Open the OneDrive app on your device.

- Check for updates in the settings or visit the OneDrive website to download the latest version of the client.

- For Windows users, go to the Microsoft Store and check for updates for OneDrive.

3. Rename Files and Folders

If you encounter syncing errors related to file or folder names, review the filenames for special characters or excessively long names. OneDrive does not support certain characters, and having them in your filenames will prevent files from syncing properly.

Solution:

- Remove any special characters like *, ?, <, >, or | from filenames.

- Shorten long file and folder names that may be causing issues.

- Rename files to ensure they comply with OneDrive's naming conventions.

4. Check Storage Space

OneDrive has a storage limit, and exceeding that limit will prevent files from syncing. Check your available storage to ensure you haven't hit your limit. If you're nearing your storage capacity, you may need to free up space or upgrade your plan.

Solution:

- Open OneDrive and check your available storage under the "Storage" section in settings.

- Delete any unnecessary files or move them to an external storage device.

- If you need more space, consider upgrading to a larger storage plan or purchasing additional storage.

5. Resolve Conflicting Versions

Conflicting versions of files can occur when changes are made on multiple devices without syncing. OneDrive will try to merge changes, but if it can't, it will create duplicate files with conflicting names.

Solution:

- Check your OneDrive folder for any duplicate files and compare the versions.

- Manually merge the changes by copying and pasting the content from one file to another.

- Rename the conflicting file versions so you can keep both versions and resolve the conflict.

6. Repair Corrupted Files

Corrupted files can be a significant cause of syncing errors. Unfortunately, once a file is corrupted, it may be impossible to recover the original file through OneDrive syncing alone.

Solution:

- Try to open the file and see if it can be repaired using the app in which it was created (e.g., Microsoft Word, Excel, etc.).

- If the file is still corrupted, try restoring it from a backup or previous version in OneDrive.

- In some cases, you may need to replace the corrupted file entirely by uploading a new version.

7. Ensure Proper Permissions

If you're having trouble syncing shared files, it could be due to permission issues. You need the appropriate permissions to sync and edit files. If you're not the owner of the file, check with the file owner to ensure you have the correct access level.

Solution:

- Contact the owner of the shared file or folder and ask them to grant you the necessary permissions.

- Ensure that you have edit permissions if you need to sync changes to the file.

8. Reinstall OneDrive

If the syncing issue persists despite all other attempts, reinstalling the OneDrive app may be the best solution. This can resolve any issues caused by corrupted app files or settings.

Solution:

- Uninstall OneDrive from your device.

- Download and reinstall the latest version of OneDrive.

- Sign in with your Microsoft account and let the app resync your files.

Conclusion

File syncing errors in OneDrive can be frustrating, but with the right troubleshooting steps, you can quickly resolve them and get back to working seamlessly across your devices. Whether the issue stems from connectivity problems, file conflicts, or permission issues, the solutions provided here should help you fix the problem. By staying on top of updates, regularly monitoring your storage, and following best practices, you can minimize the risk of syncing issues and keep your files safe and up to date across all your devices.

7.2 Helpful Tips and Tricks

7.2.1 Maximizing Storage Space

Maximizing your storage space in OneDrive is essential, especially if you use a free plan with limited storage or manage numerous files in your account. Whether you're an individual user or part of a business, following these strategies will help you organize files efficiently and make the most out of the storage you have available.

1. Identify and Delete Unnecessary Files

One of the simplest yet most effective ways to maximize storage space is to remove files you no longer need. Over time, it's easy to accumulate duplicate files, outdated documents, or temporary items. Follow these steps to declutter your OneDrive:

- **Search for Duplicates**: Use the search bar to identify files with similar names or extensions. Manually review these files and delete duplicates. Alternatively, third-party tools can help automate this process.

- **Review Shared Files**: Check the "Shared with me" section in OneDrive for files that may no longer be relevant. Since these files occupy storage space, consider removing access if they are not necessary.

- **Archive Old Data**: If certain files are outdated but might still be useful in the future, consider downloading them and storing them on an external drive or a local device.

2. Utilize the Files-On-Demand Feature

OneDrive's Files-On-Demand feature is a powerful way to manage storage space, particularly for users with limited device storage. This feature allows you to keep files in the cloud while only downloading them to your device when needed. Here's how to make the most of it:

- **Enable Files-On-Demand**: Open the OneDrive app, go to the settings menu, and activate the Files-On-Demand option. This will allow you to access your files without having them take up local storage space.

- **Mark Files as Online-Only**: Right-click on files or folders you rarely access and select "Free up space." This ensures these items remain in the cloud and don't consume space on your device.

- **Pin Frequently Used Files**: For files or folders you access regularly, use the "Always keep on this device" option to download and maintain local copies.

3. Compress Large Files

For files that take up significant space, compressing them can be a game-changer. Tools like WinRAR, 7-Zip, or built-in compression features in your operating system can reduce file sizes without compromising quality.

- **Compress Before Uploading**: Compress files into ZIP or RAR formats before uploading them to OneDrive. This reduces their overall size and frees up space.

- **Avoid Unnecessary Compression for Videos and Images**: For large media files, use specific compression tools like HandBrake for videos or TinyPNG for images, which optimize sizes without losing quality.

4. Leverage Microsoft 365 Subscription Benefits

Microsoft 365 subscribers benefit from additional storage space and advanced features. If you find your free storage insufficient, consider upgrading to a Microsoft 365 subscription:

- **Increased Storage**: A standard Microsoft 365 Personal subscription provides 1 TB of storage, while Family plans offer up to 6 TB shared among six users.

- **Advanced Features**: Subscribers can access tools like ransomware protection, advanced sharing controls, and a personal vault for sensitive files.

5. Use the Personal Vault Wisely

The Personal Vault is a secure location within OneDrive for storing sensitive documents. However, its storage count is included in your overall quota. To optimize space:

- **Limit Usage to Important Files**: Only store essential documents such as passports, contracts, and certificates in the vault.

- **Organize and Review Regularly**: Periodically review the files stored in the vault and remove any outdated or unnecessary items.

6. Optimize Image and Video Storage

Images and videos often consume the most space in OneDrive accounts. Managing these files efficiently can free up significant room:

- **Convert High-Resolution Images**: Use tools like TinyPNG or JPEGmini to compress images without compromising visible quality.

- **Streamline Videos**: Reduce the resolution of large videos if full HD or 4K isn't necessary. Tools like HandBrake can help you re-encode videos to a smaller size.

- **Use HEIC and HEVC Formats**: Modern image and video formats like HEIC (images) and HEVC (videos) are more storage-efficient than traditional formats. If your device supports these formats, convert existing files.

7. Regularly Monitor Storage Usage

Keeping an eye on your storage usage helps you proactively manage space before running out. OneDrive provides built-in tools to help:

- **Storage Metrics**: Visit the OneDrive settings page and click on "Manage Storage" to see a breakdown of space usage.

- **Clean Up the Recycle Bin**: Deleted files stay in OneDrive's Recycle Bin and continue occupying space until permanently removed. Regularly empty your Recycle Bin to free up space.

8. Take Advantage of Shared Libraries

For business users, SharePoint or Microsoft Teams might offer additional storage through shared libraries. Instead of using personal OneDrive storage for team files:

- **Move Files to Shared Libraries**: Collaborate on files in shared storage spaces rather than keeping them in your personal account.

- **Link Shared Files**: When sharing files with colleagues, consider sharing links to shared libraries rather than duplicating files in OneDrive.

9. Automate Backups to Free Space

Instead of cluttering your OneDrive account with backup files, use a dedicated backup strategy:

- **Cloud Backup Tools**: Third-party tools like Backblaze or Acronis can create backups of your files, reducing the need to use OneDrive for this purpose.

- **Archive Older Backups**: Periodically remove or archive old backups that are no longer needed.

10. Manage Email Attachments

Email attachments saved to OneDrive can take up unnecessary space. To minimize their impact:

- **Save Only Important Attachments**: Use Microsoft Outlook's integration with OneDrive to selectively save email attachments.

- **Delete Outdated Attachments**: Periodically review saved email attachments and delete outdated or redundant files.

11. Upgrade Your Storage Plan (When Necessary)

While maximizing free space is ideal, upgrading your plan might be inevitable for heavy users. Consider the following:

- **Compare Plans**: Review Microsoft's available storage plans and select one that fits your needs.

- **Periodic Upgrades**: If you temporarily require additional storage, choose plans that offer flexibility, such as monthly subscriptions.

Conclusion

Maximizing your OneDrive storage space involves a combination of decluttering, smart file management, and leveraging OneDrive's features. By following these practical tips, you can ensure your OneDrive account stays organized, efficient, and ready to handle your digital storage needs. Whether you're managing files for personal use or professional purposes, a little effort in optimizing storage goes a long way.

7.2.2 Boosting File Upload Speed

Uploading files to OneDrive can sometimes be a slow process, especially when dealing with large files, multiple uploads, or slower internet connections. To ensure smooth and efficient uploads, follow the strategies and tips outlined below. These methods will help you maximize upload speeds and reduce frustrations when working with OneDrive.

Understanding Factors That Affect Upload Speed

Before diving into solutions, it's crucial to understand what factors might be slowing down your uploads:

- **Internet Speed**: The most significant factor affecting upload speed is the speed of your internet connection. Upload bandwidth is often lower than download bandwidth for most internet service providers (ISPs).

- **File Size**: Larger files naturally take longer to upload. Files with high resolutions, such as videos or raw images, can be particularly time-consuming.

- **Network Traffic**: High traffic on your network, caused by multiple users or devices, can slow down your upload speed.

- **Device Performance**: If your device is running multiple processes or is low on resources (e.g., RAM or CPU), the upload process can be slowed down.

- **Server Load**: OneDrive servers occasionally experience high demand, which might temporarily impact upload speeds.

Tips for Boosting File Upload Speed

Here are actionable steps to enhance the speed of file uploads to OneDrive:

1. Optimize Your Internet Connection

Your internet connection is a key component in determining upload speed. Here's how to make the most of it:

- **Use a Wired Connection**: A direct Ethernet connection is often faster and more stable than Wi-Fi. Plugging your device into your router via Ethernet can significantly increase upload speeds.

- **Upgrade Your Internet Plan**: If your current upload bandwidth is insufficient for your needs, consider upgrading to a plan with higher upload speeds. Fiber-optic connections usually offer faster and more symmetrical upload and download speeds.

- **Reduce Network Traffic**: Minimize the number of devices and users on your network during uploads. For example, ask others to pause streaming or large downloads temporarily.

- **Restart Your Router**: Occasionally, routers may experience performance slowdowns. Restarting your router can help refresh the connection and improve speed.

2. Compress Large Files

Uploading large files can be time-consuming, but compressing them can speed up the process:

- **Use File Compression Tools**: Programs like WinRAR, 7-Zip, or built-in file compression tools in your operating system can reduce file sizes before uploading.

- **Split Large Files**: If compression is not sufficient, consider splitting large files into smaller parts using tools like 7-Zip. Upload the smaller files individually and reassemble them later if needed.

- **Convert File Formats**: Some file formats are inherently larger than others. For example, converting a video from .mov to .mp4 can reduce file size without significant loss of quality.

3. Schedule Uploads Strategically

Timing your uploads can also help in improving speed:

- **Upload During Off-Peak Hours**: Internet speeds tend to be faster during off-peak hours, such as early mornings or late evenings, when fewer people are using the network.

- **Avoid Server Downtime**: Check OneDrive's service status (available online) to ensure there are no ongoing issues or maintenance activities that might impact upload speeds.

4. Use the OneDrive Desktop Application

Uploading files through the OneDrive desktop app is often faster and more reliable than using the web interface:

- **Enable Selective Sync**: Sync only the folders you need to reduce the load on your device and network.

- **Pause and Resume Sync**: If the upload process slows down or gets stuck, pausing and resuming the sync can help refresh the connection.

5. Optimize Your Device for Uploads

Your computer's performance also affects upload speed. Follow these steps to ensure your device is optimized:

- **Close Unnecessary Applications**: Running multiple programs can consume resources, slowing down the upload process. Close all unnecessary apps during uploads.

- **Update Your Operating System**: Ensure your operating system is updated to the latest version, as updates often include performance improvements.

- **Run a Malware Scan**: Malware or viruses can significantly slow down your device's performance. Use antivirus software to scan and clean your system.

6. Use Cloud Upload Tools for Large Files

For very large uploads, specialized tools and services can streamline the process:

- **Microsoft Upload Tool**: Microsoft provides tools designed for efficient file uploads to OneDrive, such as AzCopy for advanced users.

- **Zip and Upload Option**: Some third-party tools integrate directly with OneDrive, allowing you to compress and upload files simultaneously.

7. Check OneDrive Settings

Adjusting OneDrive settings can also enhance upload speeds:

- **Disable Throttling**: Ensure that OneDrive is not limiting upload speeds. Go to the settings menu in the OneDrive desktop app and set the upload bandwidth to "Don't limit."

- **Optimize Sync Folder Settings**: Avoid syncing folders with a large number of small files, as this can reduce overall performance.

8. Use a Content Delivery Network (CDN)

For businesses or users frequently sharing large files:

- **Enable CDN Services**: Integrate OneDrive with a CDN to cache and distribute files more efficiently across geographic regions, reducing upload and download delays.

Monitoring and Improving Upload Efficiency

To ensure consistent performance, monitor upload progress and take proactive steps:

- **Use Task Manager**: On Windows, use Task Manager to monitor your network usage during uploads. Close processes that are consuming excessive bandwidth.

- **Track Progress**: Use the OneDrive app's progress indicator to keep track of how much has been uploaded.

- **Test Your Internet Speed**: Use online tools like Speedtest to measure upload speeds and identify potential bottlenecks.

When to Seek Technical Support

If upload speeds remain slow despite following these tips, consider contacting your ISP or Microsoft Support. They can provide insights into potential issues, such as server-side problems or network outages.

By applying these strategies, you can significantly boost file upload speeds to OneDrive, ensuring a smoother and more efficient experience. Whether you're a casual user or a professional managing large datasets, these tips will help you make the most of OneDrive's capabilities.

7.3 Frequently Asked Questions

7.3.1 Storage Limits and Upgrades

OneDrive is a versatile tool for file storage and sharing, but understanding its storage limits and how to upgrade when needed is critical to ensuring a seamless experience. This section provides an in-depth explanation of OneDrive's storage options, how to monitor your usage, and how to expand your storage capacity effectively.

Understanding OneDrive's Storage Limits

Free Plan

OneDrive offers a free plan to all users with a Microsoft account, providing 5 GB of storage at no cost. While this might be sufficient for storing basic documents, small photos, or a few video files, the free plan quickly becomes limiting for users who store large media files or frequently share files.

Paid Plans

OneDrive's paid plans are tailored to meet the needs of different users, from individuals to businesses:

- **Microsoft 365 Personal**: This plan costs approximately $6.99/month (or $69.99/year) and includes 1 TB of OneDrive storage. Additionally, it offers full access to Microsoft Office apps such as Word, Excel, and PowerPoint.

- **Microsoft 365 Family**: Priced at $9.99/month (or $99.99/year), this plan includes 1 TB of storage per user for up to 6 users. This option is ideal for families or small groups who want to share the subscription while keeping their data private.

- **Business and Enterprise Plans**: These plans vary based on organization size and needs, offering storage options from 1 TB per user to unlimited storage. Business plans also include advanced security and compliance features.

Education Plans

Educational institutions often have access to free or discounted OneDrive storage through Microsoft's educational initiatives. Students and staff should check with their institutions for eligibility.

Monitoring Your OneDrive Storage Usage

Knowing how much storage you've used and identifying large or unnecessary files is crucial to managing your OneDrive efficiently. Here's how you can check your usage:

1. **Via the OneDrive Web Interface**:

    o   Log in to your account on the OneDrive website.

    o   Click on the **Settings gear** icon in the top-right corner and select **Options**.

    o   Under the **Manage storage** section, you'll see a breakdown of your storage usage, including total space, used space, and remaining space.

2. **Using the Desktop App**:

    o   Right-click the OneDrive icon in your taskbar and select **Settings**.

    o   Navigate to the **Account** tab to view your storage details.

3. **On Mobile Apps**:

    o   Open the OneDrive app and tap the **Me** icon.

    o   Your storage usage will be displayed at the top of the screen.

4. **Identifying Large Files**:

    o   Use the **Storage Breakdown** feature in the web interface to identify large files or folders consuming significant space.

    o   Consider downloading or deleting old or unnecessary files to free up space.

How to Upgrade Your OneDrive Storage

If you find yourself running out of space, upgrading your storage plan is a simple process. Follow these steps to upgrade your OneDrive storage:

1. **Upgrade via the Web Interface**:

   - Log in to your OneDrive account.

   - Click the **Upgrade** button (usually displayed near your storage usage bar).

   - Choose a plan that fits your needs and complete the payment process.

2. **Upgrade Through Microsoft 365**:

   - Visit the **Microsoft 365 Plans** page on Microsoft's website.

   - Select a subscription plan (e.g., Personal or Family) that includes expanded OneDrive storage.

   - Follow the steps to purchase and activate the plan.

3. **Using the Mobile App**:

   - Open the OneDrive app on your mobile device.

   - Go to the **Me** tab and tap **Get more storage**.

   - Choose a plan and complete the in-app purchase.

Maximizing Your Current Storage

If upgrading isn't an immediate option, there are several ways to maximize your existing OneDrive storage:

1. **Delete Redundant Files**:

   - Regularly review and delete duplicate or obsolete files.

2. **Compress Large Files**:

   - Use file compression tools to reduce the size of large files before uploading them to OneDrive.

3. **Offload Non-Essential Files**:

- o Transfer rarely accessed files to external hard drives or other cloud services.

4. **Use OneDrive's Free Storage Promotions**:

- o Occasionally, Microsoft offers bonus storage promotions, such as rewards for referring new users. Check your account periodically for such offers.

Upgrading to Unlimited Storage for Businesses

Businesses with high storage demands can opt for unlimited storage, offered in certain Microsoft 365 Enterprise plans. This is particularly useful for organizations storing large datasets or managing collaborative projects requiring extensive file sharing.

To activate unlimited storage:

- Start with the default 1 TB per user.
- Request additional storage through Microsoft Admin Center as your needs grow.

Troubleshooting Storage-Related Issues

If you experience problems with storage limits or upgrades, here are some common issues and solutions:

1. **Exceeded Storage Limit**:

- o If you reach your limit, OneDrive will restrict uploads and syncing. Delete unnecessary files or upgrade your plan to resolve this.

2. **Upgrade Not Reflecting Immediately**:

- o After purchasing a plan, it might take a few hours for the new storage to appear. Log out and log back in to refresh your account.

3. **Payment Issues**:

- o Double-check your payment method or contact Microsoft Support for assistance if your payment fails.

4. **Mismatched Plan Details**:

   o Verify that you've selected the correct plan for your needs. For example, some plans include Office apps but might not provide additional storage.

Tips for Choosing the Right Plan

1. **Assess Your Storage Needs**:

   o Evaluate your current and anticipated storage requirements. For example, photographers or videographers often need larger plans.

2. **Consider Collaboration Features**:

   o If you frequently collaborate with others, a Microsoft 365 plan with integrated Office apps might be more cost-effective.

3. **Plan for Future Growth**:

   o Choose a plan with some buffer space to accommodate unexpected storage increases.

4. **Evaluate Alternative Storage Options**:

   o Compare OneDrive plans with other cloud services like Google Drive or Dropbox to ensure you're getting the best value.

By understanding the storage options, monitoring usage, and upgrading as needed, you can ensure your OneDrive experience is smooth and hassle-free. Whether you're a casual user or a business professional, OneDrive has flexible solutions to meet your needs, making it a cornerstone of your digital organization strategy.

7.3.2 Resolving File Access Conflicts

File access conflicts can occur in OneDrive when multiple users edit the same file simultaneously, or when the same file is updated on different devices without proper syncing. These conflicts are common in collaborative environments or when offline edits are made. Below, we will explore the causes of file access conflicts, ways to resolve them, and preventive measures to avoid future conflicts.

Understanding File Access Conflicts

File access conflicts typically arise when:

1. **Simultaneous Edits:** Multiple users edit the same file at the same time without using co-authoring features.

2. **Sync Delays:** A device does not sync changes to the OneDrive cloud in real time, leading to multiple versions of the same file.

3. **Offline Changes:** Files are edited offline on different devices and later uploaded to OneDrive. The system cannot merge changes automatically, resulting in conflict files.

4. **File Locks:** Some applications lock files while editing, preventing other users from accessing them.

When a conflict arises, OneDrive often creates duplicate files labeled with a timestamp or the editor's name, such as *"Document (1) – User's Name"*. This ensures that no data is lost but can lead to confusion when managing multiple versions.

Steps to Resolve File Access Conflicts

Step 1: Identify the Conflict Files

1. Open the OneDrive folder where the conflict occurred.

2. Look for files with names that include additional labels, such as:

   o *"Conflict Copy"*

   o *"Modified by [User]"*

   o Timestamps, such as *"FileName (1) – 2024-12-25"*.

3. Compare the conflict file with the original file to understand the changes.

Step 2: Review Changes

1. Open both versions of the file side by side to analyze differences.

    o For text documents, use the "Track Changes" feature in Microsoft Word or Google Docs.

    o For spreadsheets, review formulas and data modifications in Excel.

2. Take note of edits made by each user or on each device.

Step 3: Merge the Changes

1. If the changes are minimal, manually copy and paste updates from one file into the other.

2. For extensive changes, follow these steps:

    o Open the primary version of the file in the application (e.g., Word, Excel).

    o Use the *Compare and Merge* tool, if available, to integrate differences.

    o Save the file with a unified version number or name, such as *"FinalVersion_25Dec2024"*.

Step 4: Delete Duplicate Files

Once the conflict is resolved and all changes are merged, remove duplicate versions to avoid confusion. However, keep a backup in case additional edits are needed later.

Resolving Common Conflict Scenarios

Scenario 1: Edits from Multiple Users

When multiple users edit a shared file, OneDrive may save separate versions for each editor. To resolve this:

1. Inform team members to use co-authoring features in Office apps to avoid future conflicts.

2. Merge edits manually or with document comparison tools.

3. Communicate a clear process for file editing, such as locking files or assigning editing windows.

Scenario 2: Offline Edits

Offline edits often lead to conflicts when changes are re-uploaded to OneDrive. Resolve this by:

1. Synchronizing the device with OneDrive before starting any edits.

2. Reviewing both offline and cloud versions to determine differences.

3. Merging changes using the steps outlined above.

Scenario 3: Syncing Delays

If syncing delays result in conflict files:

1. Pause and restart OneDrive syncing to refresh the connection.

2. Check for updates to the OneDrive app to ensure optimal performance.

3. Use the OneDrive web version to upload and review files manually if syncing fails.

Preventing File Access Conflicts

Tip 1: Enable Real-Time Collaboration

1. Use Microsoft Office apps for real-time collaboration.

   o Co-authoring allows multiple users to edit the same document simultaneously without creating conflicts.

   o Changes are saved instantly to the cloud.

2. Inform team members to always use the cloud version of OneDrive for editing shared files.

Tip 2: Regularly Sync Your Devices

1. Always connect your device to the internet before making edits.

2. Verify that OneDrive has synced your latest changes by checking the sync status icon.

Tip 3: Use Clear File Naming Conventions

1. Avoid generic names like *"Document1"* or *"FinalVersion"*.

2. Adopt version control practices by including dates or version numbers in file names. For example:

    o *"ProjectPlan_v1"*

    o *"SalesReport_2024-12-25"*.

Tip 4: Set Permissions Carefully

1. Assign editing rights only to necessary users to limit conflicting changes.

2. Encourage users with view-only access to download copies for personal edits.

Tip 5: Educate Team Members

1. Train team members on the best practices for shared file management.

2. Use tools like Microsoft Teams or email reminders to notify users about shared file updates.

Using OneDrive Tools to Manage Conflicts

Version History

1. Right-click the conflict file in OneDrive and select *Version History*.

2. Review all previous versions to identify which one contains the desired changes.

3. Restore the correct version or save a copy for merging.

Activity Feed

1. Access the activity feed in OneDrive to see who made changes and when.

2. Use this information to trace the source of conflicts and communicate with collaborators.

Microsoft Support Options

1. Use the OneDrive help center for conflict resolution guides.

2. Contact Microsoft Support if conflicts persist and require advanced troubleshooting.

Case Study: Resolving a Real-World Conflict

Imagine a scenario where three team members edit a shared budget spreadsheet offline while traveling. When they reconnect to the internet, OneDrive creates three conflict versions of the file.

1. Each user uploads their version of the spreadsheet.

2. The team leader compares the changes using Excel's *Compare and Merge* feature.

3. A unified file is created, and the conflict copies are archived for reference.

4. Team members agree to always use real-time editing going forward.

Conclusion

Resolving file access conflicts in OneDrive may seem daunting, but by following the steps outlined above, you can efficiently manage and merge conflicting changes. Adopting preventive measures like real-time collaboration, regular syncing, and clear communication will help minimize future conflicts, ensuring smooth teamwork and organized file management.

Conclusion

8.1 Recap of Key Takeaways

As we conclude our journey through the ins and outs of OneDrive, it's important to revisit the essential lessons and concepts covered throughout this guide. Whether you're a beginner just starting with OneDrive or someone looking to enhance your knowledge, these key takeaways will serve as a quick reference and reminder of the power and utility of this tool. Let's summarize the most important aspects of what you've learned.

The Basics of OneDrive

At its core, **OneDrive** is a cloud-based storage solution designed to simplify how you store, access, and manage your files. From understanding the differences between free and paid plans to setting up your account, you've gained insights into the foundational aspects of using OneDrive effectively:

- **Ease of Access:** Files stored in OneDrive can be accessed anytime, anywhere, and on any device. This level of accessibility ensures you are never tied down by physical devices.

- **Interface Familiarity:** Navigating the OneDrive interface is simple once you understand the layout of the desktop application, web version, and mobile app. Each platform offers unique features tailored to specific needs.

Uploading and Organizing Files

OneDrive's organization features are crucial for keeping your files structured and easy to find. Here's what we covered:

- **Uploading Files and Folders:** You've learned how to add files to OneDrive via drag-and-drop or upload buttons. Large files can be easily stored without worrying about physical device limitations.

- **Creating Folders:** A well-structured folder system helps prevent clutter and improves productivity. Naming conventions and thoughtful organization are key.

- **Search and Sorting Tools:** Using advanced search filters ensures that you can locate files even when you're dealing with large volumes of data.

Sharing and Collaboration

Collaboration is one of OneDrive's standout features, enabling teams and individuals to work seamlessly together:

- **File Sharing Options:** You've mastered generating shareable links, setting permissions, and sharing folders securely.

- **Real-Time Collaboration:** The ability to co-author documents ensures efficient teamwork, particularly when using Microsoft Office applications.

- **Managing Shared Content:** Keeping track of who has access to your files and adjusting permissions ensures your data remains secure while fostering collaboration.

Syncing and Offline Access

OneDrive's syncing capabilities allow for seamless integration across devices:

- **Sync Setup:** By selecting specific folders to sync, you've optimized both your local storage and cloud usage.

- **Offline Access:** You now know how to enable offline mode, edit files without an internet connection, and sync changes automatically when you're back online.

- **Troubleshooting Sync Issues:** Understanding how to resolve common syncing errors ensures a smooth experience.

Advanced Features

Beyond the basics, OneDrive offers several advanced features to elevate your productivity:

- **Microsoft Office Integration:** By saving documents directly to OneDrive and accessing them through Office apps, your workflow becomes smoother.

- **Third-Party Tool Integration:** From Microsoft Teams to third-party applications, OneDrive enhances compatibility across platforms.

- **Automation and Workflows:** Automating tasks, such as file backups and sharing workflows, helps streamline repetitive processes.

Security and Privacy

Data security is a top priority, and OneDrive equips you with tools to protect your files:

- **Encryption and Two-Factor Authentication:** Ensuring your account and data are protected against unauthorized access.

- **Privacy Controls:** You've learned how to configure account permissions and monitor access logs to keep track of who interacts with your files.

- **Best Practices:** Implementing strong passwords and avoiding phishing attacks adds an extra layer of security to your cloud storage.

Troubleshooting and FAQs

Finally, we covered common issues and provided practical solutions to help you overcome hurdles:

- **Login and Syncing Problems:** These are among the most frequent challenges faced by users, and now you know how to address them.

- **Maximizing Storage Space:** You've explored strategies like deleting unnecessary files and upgrading storage plans to ensure you have enough space for your needs.

Practical Applications

The key takeaways above are more than just theoretical knowledge—they're tools you can apply to your daily life. Here's a quick recap of how OneDrive enhances various aspects of file management:

- **Personal Use:** Store family photos, important documents, and personal projects securely and access them from anywhere.

- **Professional Use:** Collaborate with colleagues on shared projects, manage workflows, and integrate OneDrive into your organization's digital ecosystem.

- **Educational Use:** Keep assignments, research papers, and educational resources organized for easy retrieval.

Looking Forward

OneDrive is constantly evolving, with Microsoft regularly introducing new features to enhance user experience. As you continue your journey with OneDrive, remember to stay updated on these changes. Whether it's improved AI-powered search, deeper integration with other tools, or enhanced security measures, there's always more to explore.

In the next sections, we'll discuss practical steps you can take to deepen your OneDrive expertise and prepare for future updates. Stay tuned as we dive into how to maximize your potential with this powerful tool!

8.2 Next Steps with OneDrive

Now that you've familiarized yourself with OneDrive's features and capabilities, it's time to think about how to incorporate it into your personal or professional workflow effectively. The key to maximizing the benefits of OneDrive lies in not only using its current features but also planning for how you can adapt to its evolving functionalities in the future. This section will guide you through actionable next steps to deepen your usage of OneDrive, optimize your file management system, and integrate the tool into your broader digital ecosystem.

8.2.1 Setting Long-Term File Management Goals

Effective file management is not just about storing and sharing documents; it's about creating a structured system that grows with your needs. Consider the following approaches to set long-term goals for using OneDrive:

1. **Define Folder Structures for Scalability**:

   Organize your folders in a way that they can easily accommodate future growth. For instance, if you're managing personal files, categorize them into major life areas such as "Work," "Finance," "Family," or "Projects." For professional use, consider client-based or project-based folders, ensuring that the naming conventions are clear and consistent.

2. **Regularly Review and Clean Up Files**:

   Schedule periodic reviews of your OneDrive account to declutter unnecessary files, rename outdated documents, and archive completed projects. Tools like tags and metadata can help categorize files, making them easier to retrieve when needed.

3. **Set File Naming Conventions**:

   Create a naming convention to ensure consistency across your files. For example, include dates or project codes in file names to make sorting and searching more efficient.

4. **Utilize OneDrive's Versioning System**:

Incorporate file versioning into your workflow. Before making major edits to shared documents, save a version history so you can easily roll back if needed.

8.2.2 Expanding Collaboration Opportunities

OneDrive is an exceptional tool for collaboration, and leveraging its capabilities can transform the way you work with teams, clients, or classmates. Here's how you can take your collaboration efforts to the next level:

1. **Onboard Your Team to OneDrive**:

   If your organization isn't fully utilizing OneDrive, consider introducing it as a team collaboration tool. Host a brief workshop to showcase how shared folders, file permissions, and co-authoring features can streamline team workflows.

2. **Integrate with Microsoft Teams**:

   Take advantage of OneDrive's seamless integration with Microsoft Teams for real-time collaboration. Shared OneDrive links can be embedded directly into Teams channels, ensuring everyone has quick access to the same resources.

3. **Improve Document Reviews with Commenting**:

   When working on collaborative projects, use OneDrive's commenting features to leave feedback directly on documents. This eliminates the need for back-and-forth emails and keeps all discussions tied to the relevant file.

4. **Leverage Shared Libraries for Long-Term Projects**:

   For ongoing collaborations, set up shared libraries through SharePoint or OneDrive for Business. This approach centralizes file management and ensures that everyone always has access to the latest versions.

8.2.3 Automating Processes with OneDrive

Automation is a powerful way to save time and reduce repetitive tasks. By integrating OneDrive with automation tools, you can streamline workflows and focus on higher-value activities.

1. **Use Power Automate for Workflow Automation**:

   Power Automate (formerly Microsoft Flow) allows you to create workflows that connect OneDrive with other apps and services. Examples include automatically saving email attachments to a designated OneDrive folder or sending notifications when a file is updated.

2. **Schedule Regular Backups**:

   Automate backups of essential files from your local device or other cloud services to OneDrive. This ensures that your data is protected and readily available in case of a system failure.

3. **Sync with Third-Party Tools**:

   Many third-party tools like Zapier or IFTTT (If This Then That) offer integration options for OneDrive. For instance, you can set up triggers to save social media posts or create logs in OneDrive for specific actions performed in other platforms.

4. **Set Up File Requests**:

   Use OneDrive's file request feature to automate the collection of documents from others, such as client contracts, homework submissions, or team reports.

8.2.4 Deepening Your Integration with Microsoft 365

As part of the Microsoft 365 ecosystem, OneDrive offers unparalleled integration with other tools in the suite. Here are some ways to further incorporate it into your daily activities:

1. **Connect with Outlook for Seamless Attachments**:

   Instead of attaching files directly to emails, use OneDrive links in Outlook. This not only reduces email size but also allows recipients to view the latest versions of your files.

2. **Embed Files in Word, Excel, and PowerPoint**:

Work directly from your OneDrive account when creating or editing documents in Word, Excel, or PowerPoint. This ensures that your files are saved and accessible from anywhere.

3. **Link with Microsoft Planner for Project Management**:

Attach OneDrive files to tasks in Microsoft Planner to keep your project documentation and task tracking in one place.

4. **Streamline Meetings with Microsoft Teams**:

Share meeting agendas, presentations, and notes via OneDrive links in Microsoft Teams. This ensures that everyone has access to updated materials before and after the meeting.

8.2.5 Preparing for Future Features and Updates

OneDrive is constantly evolving, with Microsoft regularly adding new features and improving existing ones. To stay ahead, adopt the following practices:

1. **Follow Official Microsoft Channels**:

Keep up with announcements and updates by following the official Microsoft OneDrive blog or subscribing to newsletters. This ensures you're aware of any new capabilities as soon as they're released.

2. **Join User Communities**:

Participate in OneDrive forums or Microsoft 365 user groups to exchange tips and learn how others are using new features.

3. **Experiment with Beta Features**:

If available, sign up for beta programs to test new OneDrive features before they're widely released. This gives you a chance to adapt your workflows early.

4. **Invest in Training and Certifications**:

Consider enrolling in Microsoft's online training programs or earning certifications to deepen your expertise with OneDrive and related tools.

8.2.6 Promoting Digital Literacy

Finally, consider sharing your knowledge of OneDrive with others to promote digital literacy. This not only reinforces your understanding but also helps colleagues, friends, or family members become more organized and efficient. You can:

1. **Host Workshops or Tutorials**:

   Organize training sessions for your team or community to demonstrate how to use OneDrive effectively.

2. **Create How-To Guides or Videos**:

   Publish tutorials or videos showcasing specific tips and tricks for OneDrive users.

3. **Offer Ongoing Support**:

   Be a resource for others by answering questions and sharing updates about OneDrive's features and best practices.

By following these next steps, you'll not only maximize the value you get from OneDrive but also position yourself as a knowledgeable and efficient user of cloud storage solutions. Embracing OneDrive's evolving features and integrating it further into your workflows will ensure that you stay organized, productive, and ready for the digital future.

8.3 Staying Updated with Future Features

OneDrive, as part of Microsoft's suite of cloud-based services, is constantly evolving to meet the needs of its users. Staying informed about new features, updates, and enhancements ensures that you can continue to use OneDrive efficiently and leverage its full potential. This chapter focuses on practical steps, tools, and strategies for staying up-to-date with OneDrive's future developments, ensuring you remain at the forefront of cloud storage technology.

Understanding the Importance of Updates

OneDrive updates are more than just aesthetic changes or bug fixes; they often introduce critical features that enhance productivity, security, and collaboration. Microsoft continually invests in research and development to improve user experience. For example, past updates have introduced AI-powered search, enhanced security protocols, and better integrations with Microsoft Teams and other Office 365 applications. By staying updated, you not only benefit from these innovations but also ensure compatibility with other Microsoft tools you may use.

Microsoft's Communication Channels

Microsoft employs several platforms to announce and discuss new OneDrive features. Here are the primary channels to monitor:

1. **Microsoft 365 Blog**

   The Microsoft 365 Blog is the official source for news, updates, and announcements related to OneDrive and other Microsoft services. Subscribing to this blog ensures you receive timely information about feature rollouts, tips, and upcoming developments.

   o **How to Access**: Visit https://www.microsoft.com/en-us/microsoft-365/blog/.

- o **Content Examples**: New feature announcements, best practices, and product roadmaps.

2. **OneDrive UserVoice (Feedback Portal)**

Microsoft values user feedback, and its UserVoice platform often serves as a preview of potential features based on community demand. Users can vote on ideas, providing insight into what might be prioritized for future updates.

- o **How to Access**: Go to https://feedbackportal.microsoft.com/.

- o **Usefulness**: Track suggestions that Microsoft plans to implement or refine.

3. **Microsoft Tech Community**

The Tech Community forum is an excellent place to engage with other users, IT professionals, and Microsoft employees. Discussions often include upcoming changes and how users are preparing for them.

- o **How to Access**: Visit https://techcommunity.microsoft.com/.

- o **Tip**: Join the "OneDrive" group to focus on relevant topics.

4. **Release Notes and Updates Page**

Microsoft maintains a detailed page for release notes and updates, summarizing changes made to OneDrive. This resource is invaluable for IT administrators and advanced users looking to understand the specifics of each update.

- o **How to Access**: Check the OneDrive section of the Microsoft 365 updates page.

- o **Frequency**: Updated monthly or as needed.

Using the Microsoft 365 Roadmap

The Microsoft 365 Roadmap is a dynamic resource that outlines upcoming features, the development process, and expected release dates for OneDrive and other tools. It allows you to plan and adapt your workflows in anticipation of new features.

1. **Understanding the Roadmap**

- o **Categories**: Features are grouped by "In Development," "Rolling Out," and "Launched."

- o **Filters**: Use filters to focus on OneDrive-specific updates or other tools relevant to your workflow.

2. **Benefits of Monitoring**

- o Gain early awareness of upcoming changes.

- o Prepare your team or personal workflow for feature integrations.

3. **Practical Example**

If a new security protocol is listed as "Rolling Out," you can start researching how it might impact your current sharing settings and train your team in advance.

Leveraging In-App Notifications

OneDrive itself is an excellent resource for updates. Microsoft often uses in-app notifications to alert users to new features or changes. These notifications typically appear as pop-ups or banners within the desktop app, web interface, or mobile application.

1. **Desktop App Notifications**

- o When a feature update is released, the desktop app may guide you through a brief tutorial or highlight the change.

- o Example: When the "Personal Vault" feature was introduced, OneDrive displayed an interactive walkthrough.

2. **Mobile App Notifications**

- o The mobile app occasionally pushes notifications about new tools or updates.

- o Tip: Enable notifications for the OneDrive app to stay informed.

3. **Web Interface Announcements**

  o Updates are often highlighted on the OneDrive homepage under banners or in the "What's New" section.

Engaging with Training Resources

Microsoft provides extensive training materials to help users adapt to changes. These resources are particularly helpful for learning how to implement new features effectively.

1. **Microsoft Learn Platform**

   The Microsoft Learn platform offers free tutorials, articles, and interactive modules about OneDrive and other products.

    o **Example Topics**: "Using Advanced Sharing Options in OneDrive," "Optimizing Storage with AI Recommendations."

    o **Link**: https://learn.microsoft.com/.

2. **YouTube Tutorials**

   The official Microsoft YouTube channel frequently posts demonstrations of new features. Subscribing to this channel ensures you can visually see how updates are implemented.

    o **Tip**: Watch community-driven tutorials as well, which often explore creative uses of OneDrive features.

3. **Workshops and Webinars**

    o Microsoft occasionally hosts live sessions or webinars focusing on new updates.

    o Example: "Mastering Collaboration with OneDrive and Teams" webinar.

Adapting to Changes in Workflow

As OneDrive evolves, it's important to adapt your workflows to integrate new features. Here's a structured approach:

1. **Assess Relevance**

   Not all updates may apply to your needs. For example, an enterprise-focused feature might not benefit personal users.

2. **Test Before Implementation**

   For significant updates, create a test environment or use a dummy account to explore the feature without risking your existing data or workflows.

3. **Train Your Team**

   Share documentation or host mini-training sessions for your team to ensure everyone understands and uses new features effectively.

Future Trends to Anticipate

Microsoft's innovation roadmap often includes broader trends in technology. Here are some potential areas where OneDrive is likely to see development:

1. **AI and Machine Learning**

   o Smarter file recommendations based on usage patterns.

   o Enhanced search capabilities using AI to recognize file contents.

2. **Tighter Integrations**

   o Deeper connections with tools like Microsoft Loop and Copilot.

   o Cross-platform functionality for hybrid workplaces.

3. **Enhanced Security**

   o Improved encryption technologies.

   o Biometric authentication options for enterprise users.

4. **Sustainability Features**

   o Tools to monitor the environmental impact of file storage and operations.

Building a Habit of Staying Updated

Finally, staying updated with OneDrive doesn't have to be overwhelming. Make it a habit by scheduling regular check-ins on Microsoft's update channels or subscribing to newsletters. By doing so, you'll always be prepared to take full advantage of what OneDrive has to offer.

This proactive approach to staying informed about OneDrive ensures you maximize your investment in the platform and stay ahead in your personal or professional workflows. Whether you're using OneDrive for personal file management, business collaboration, or creative projects, understanding and leveraging its latest features will empower you to work smarter and more efficiently.

Acknowledgments

First and foremost, I want to express my heartfelt gratitude to you, the reader, for choosing this book, *OneDrive Essentials: Manage Your Files with Ease*. Your time and effort in exploring the world of OneDrive through these pages mean everything to me. This book was written with the hope of making your journey with OneDrive simpler, more efficient, and more empowering, and I'm honored that you entrusted me to guide you.

To everyone who has supported this project along the way, thank you. To the incredible team at Microsoft who continually innovates and develops tools like OneDrive that make our lives easier, your work is deeply appreciated.

A special thanks to my family, friends, and colleagues for their encouragement and patience throughout the writing process. Your belief in my vision kept me motivated and inspired.

Lastly, this book wouldn't exist without the feedback, questions, and ideas from individuals like you. If you've learned something new, streamlined your workflow, or felt empowered through this guide, then this book has achieved its purpose.

I encourage you to stay curious, keep exploring, and embrace the possibilities that technology offers. If you have any feedback or stories about how OneDrive has transformed your productivity, I would love to hear from you.

Thank you for being part of this journey. Here's to organizing, sharing, and thriving in the cloud!

Warm regards,